bONSAI
a care manual

Colin Lewis

LAUREL
GLEN

San Diego, California

Publishing Director
Laura Bamford
Executive Editor
Julian Brown
Assistant Editor
Karen O'Grady
Executive Art Editor
Mark Winwood
Art Director
Keith Martin
Photography
Peter Myers
and Michael Gomez
Production Controller
Melanie Frantz
Picture Research
Liz Fowler

Laurel Glen Publishing
An imprint of the Advantage
Publishers Group
5880 Oberlin Drive, San Diego
CA 92121-4794
www.laurelglenbooks.com

Copyright © 1997 Octopus
Publishing Group Limited

ISBN 1-57145-988-X

Library of Congress
Cataloging-in-Publication Data
available upon request.

Printed in China
Produced by Toppan

1 2 3 4 5 06 05 04 03 02

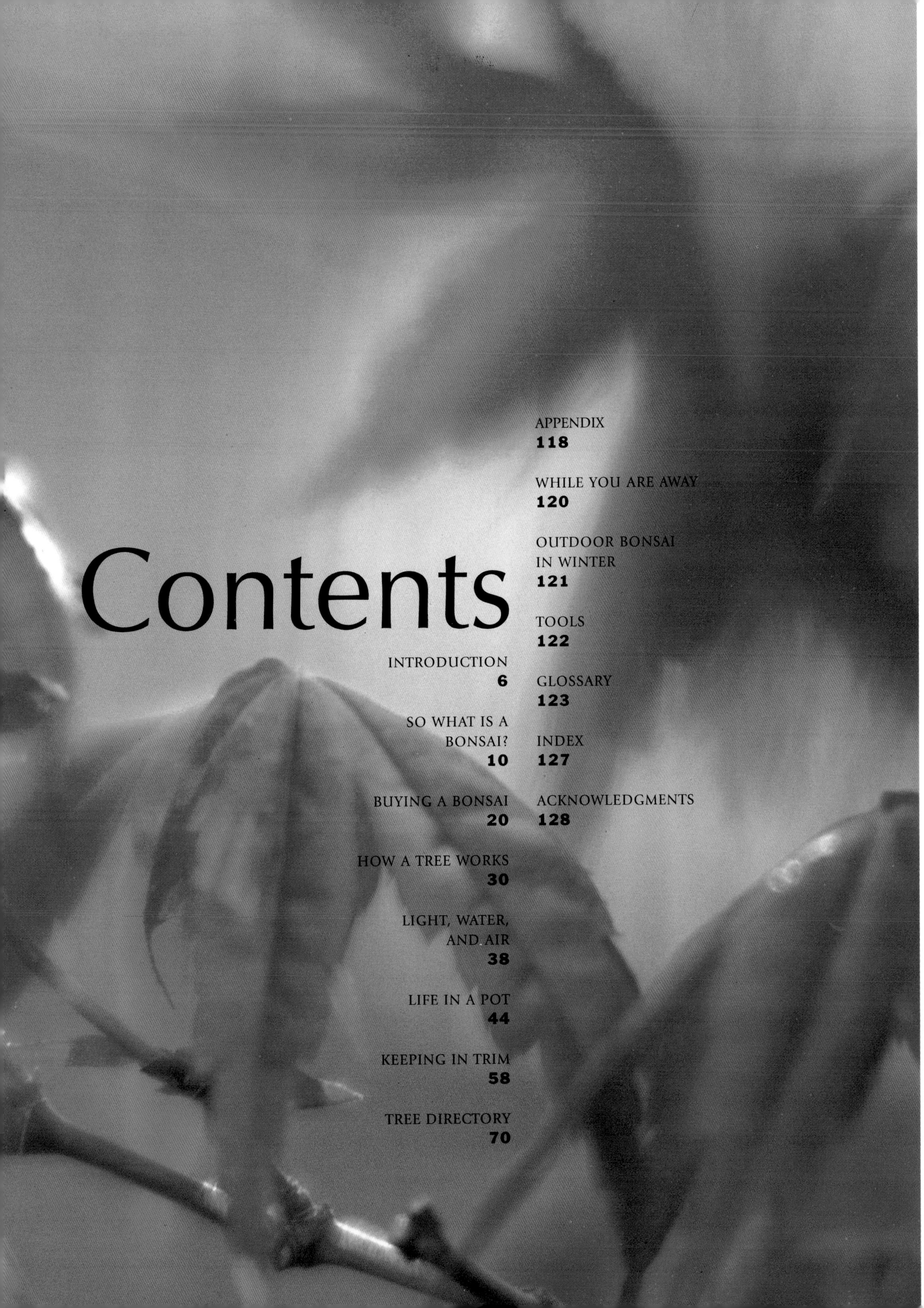

Contents

INTRODUCTION
6

SO WHAT IS A
BONSAI?
10

BUYING A BONSAI
20

HOW A TREE WORKS
30

LIGHT, WATER,
AND AIR
38

LIFE IN A POT
44

KEEPING IN TRIM
58

TREE DIRECTORY
70

APPENDIX
118

WHILE YOU ARE AWAY
120

OUTDOOR BONSAI
IN WINTER
121

TOOLS
122

GLOSSARY
123

INDEX
127

ACKNOWLEDGMENTS
128

Introduction

For most people, their first encounter with bonsai is probably in a department store or garden nursery during the pre-Christmas shopping panic. Each year many thousands of little trees are imported from China, Japan, and other Far Eastern countries to satisfy the gift market. Sadly, most of these will die – either through neglect or, ironically, more often through excessive care by their enthusiastic new owners. This fact is all the more sad because the initial disappointment often deters the novice from progressing further, and an opportunity to develop a thoroughly rewarding and satisfying new hobby is lost.

In fact, keeping a bonsai alive and healthy is not significantly more difficult than caring for any other potted plant, provided you understand the difference between an ordinary plant pot and a shallow bonsai container, and you are aware of the requirements of the particular species in question. The watering, feeding, and pruning of bonsai are straightforward gardening techniques which can be learned easily and quickly, even by someone with no prior experience in dealing with plants.

The practical skills required to maintain and develop the shape of a bonsai are also very easy to acquire. Pruning roots and branches, pinching out growing shoots, and shaping branches with wire are all simple techniques which are identical to those employed by the most revered Japanese masters. Once learned, they are never forgotten and will enable you to progress in your bonsai hobby as far as you want.

Of course, you may be content with just one or two bonsai to decorate your home or garden. But the chances are that you will be so fascinated by the challenge and reward of cultivating miniaturized trees that you will, in time, become totally hooked. Your collection will grow and your thirst for more detailed and advanced knowledge will grow with it. You may seek the advice of more experienced bonsaiists you meet at your local nursery, or you may subscribe to some of the specialty magazines that are now available. But by far the best way to progress is to join a local club or study group.

Bonsai clubs provide their members with visiting teachers, lecturers, practical workshops, libraries, and many other learning aids. But the most valuable asset of all is the contact you will have with other like-minded bonsai enthusiasts of all levels of ability and experience. They will always be ready to offer advice and guidance and, before you know it, you too will be advising new members who come to their first meeting bursting with questions.

One final point. It is always worth remembering that even the top Japanese and Chinese bonsai masters were once beginners themselves, ignorant of the techniques this art form requires. Many of them had to learn the hard way – through trial and error, and by experiment. Their wisdom has been passed on to others, in the East and the West, and is now available to you through the pages of this book, enabling you to gain the knowledge you will need quickly and easily.

Colin Lewis

So what is a bonsai?

So, what is a bonsai?

Perhaps it is better to start by explaining what a bonsai is not. A bonsai is not a genetically dwarfed plant; it is not treated with magic potions to reduce its size, and above all, it is not kept small by cruelty in any way. In fact, given an adequate supply of water, air, light, and nutrients, a properly maintained bonsai should outlive a full-size tree of the same species (*see Chapter Three*).

Literally translated from Japanese, the term "bonsai" means a tree in a pot. But over the centuries the definition has come to mean a lot more. To begin with, the tree and the pot form a single harmonious unit where the shape, texture, and color of one compliments the other. Then the tree must be shaped. It is not enough just to plant a tree in a pot and allow nature to take its course – the result would look nothing like a tree and would be very short-lived. Every branch and twig of a bonsai is shaped or eliminated until the chosen image is achieved. From then on, the image is maintained and improved by a constant regime of pruning and trimming.

At all times, a bonsai must be kept in perfect condition. A bonsai can't outgrow an infestation of aphids in the same way a wild tree can. Neither can it send out long roots to search for water in periods of dry weather, and it doesn't receive a regular supply of nutrients from animals and decaying vegetation. A bonsai depends

Opposite: The shape of the white pine bonsai and the decoration on the pot indicate the strong Chinese influence on Japanese culture of this period

entirely on its current owner for all these things. But don't be deterred; it is not as difficult as it sounds. Remember the literal meaning of bonsai – a tree in a pot. Although a little more time-consuming, a modest bonsai should be no more difficult to care for than any other type of potted plant.

In The Beginning...

Mankind has been growing plants in containers for thousands of years, normally for culinary or medicinal purposes, but only very rarely for their beauty. When plants were containerized for decoration it was because of their flowers or foliage. But on one occasion, probably in China, a new concept was born – that of creating miniature representations of natural landscapes in containers. Wall paintings dating back to the Han dynasty, around 200 BC, show such landscapes, complete with trees, rocks, and grasses, being carried by servants. Nowadays, over 2,000 years later, these *penjing* still constitute a major part of bonsai culture in China and other Far Eastern countries.

There are many legends about the spiritual significance of penjing, most involving powerful emperors or fiery dragons. One favorite suggests that an overweight emperor found traveling tiresome, so he demanded that a miniature replica of his empire should be built in his courtyard to enable him to survey his entire domain from the bedroom window. We will never know the truth, but it certainly is true that for hundreds of years ownership of a miniature containerized landscape was a considerable status symbol.

The practice of growing single specimen trees in pots came later, again in China, but exactly when is a mystery. These early specimens displayed sparse foliage and rugged, gnarled trunks which often looked like animals or birds. These were called *pun-sai*, the root of the Japanese word *bonsai*, and were the forerunners of the million or more small, commercial "indoor bonsai" exported from China each year.

Bonsai in Japan

During the 11th and 12th centuries there was considerable cultural movement between China and its neighbors, particularly the Japanese, who readily adopted much of Chinese art and philosophy. Perhaps the most significant influence was the Chinese Zen religion, whose monks played a leading role in introducing bonsai to the Japanese ruling classes.

Bonsai rapidly became entrenched in Japanese culture and seems to have been practiced both on a spiritual and aesthetic level. While the Buddhist monks adopted the intellectual, abstract approach, there is considerable evidence that as early as the late 13th century stunted wild trees were collected and trained as bonsai by ordinary citizens. Specialist techniques also began to develop at this time, although, as the poet Yoshida Kenko suggested in his *Essays in Idleness*, c. 1330, the results were not always successful and tended towards deformity rather than beauty. He regarded bonsai as unnatural and once compared them to beggars with twisted limbs. The same argument continues to rage today, wherever bonsai are grown.

Right: This zelkova, otherwise known as the Gray bark elm (*Zelkova serrata*) already looks like a miniature tree, yet it won't cost a fortune

Below: A Japanese master at work

Development of modern bonsai

Bonsai, like all leisure activities, has been subjected to changes in fashion over the years. For example in the mid-17th Century the passion was for camellias, then azaleas. Each year new varieties were exhibited at the equivalent of modern flower shows. One document records 162 new varieties of azalea and 200 camellias. At one point the obsession with variegated plants was so strong that the artistic approach

Above: Specimen Japanese black pine in all its glory. Trees of this stature are quite expensive and are for serious collectors only!

Left: The Japanese characters for "bonsai" are still identical to the Chinese

to bonsai was almost completely lost in the frantic search for new leaf patterns and colors.

However, it survived, and during the Edo period (1603-1868) became truly established as a highly refined artistic discipline. The techniques became ritualized and the shapes and placement of the branches and trunks governed by a very strict code. Several manuals were produced detailing the exact requirements of the ideal bonsai and giving extremely precise horticultural instructions.

By the late 19th Century bonsai had become an industry, with many professional artists and commercial growers supplying an ever-increasing demand

Bonsai in the West

There are records of early Victorian travelers returning from the Orient telling stories of bizarre little trees, with intentionally bent and twisted branches, apparently clinging to life in ceramic containers. But it was not until the Paris Exhibition in 1878 that bonsai were appreciated by the Western public. The display in the Japanese Pavilion won a gold medal and brought bonsai to the attention of the European middle classes.

Classic Japanese bonsai follow clearly defined styles which are based on idealized images of natural tree-forms. The story each one tells is of the tree itself and the environment it lives in.

at all levels of society. In 1892 the first Artistic Bonsai Concourse was held in a Tokyo restaurant, and in 1928 the first of the current series of Kokufu-ten exhibitions was held in the Metropolitan Art Museum in Tokyo.

Japanese and Chinese styles

While bonsai in Japan was undergoing centuries of development and refinement which was producing increasingly simplified and, to the westerner, arguably more aesthetic results, in China the only significant change was that bonsai became more populist in its appeal. There are a great number of myths and legends surrounding Chinese bonsai, and the grotesque or animal-like trunks and root formations are still highly prized today. Chinese bonsai come from the landscape of the imagination and images of fiery dragons and coiled serpents take far greater precedence over images of trees.

Above: The animal-like roots of this Sageretia are typical of Chinese specimen bonsai

Right: This little pistachio would be a good, inexpensive tree for the novice to learn on

Ironically, it was as a result of World War Two that bonsai became the internationally popular pastime it is today. Servicemen and diplomats returning from tours of duty in Japan brought back examples as souvenirs. Some people took time to learn about their care before leaving Japan, and a few of these original imports are still alive today. In the United States the large expatriot Japanese population in California provided the vital link between the energetic, enthusiastic Westerner with time on his hands and the traditional Japanese wisdom built over the centuries.

Nowadays bonsai is practiced all over the world, and the different cultures, climates, and species of each country have prompted the development of new styles and techniques. The Port Jackson figs of Australia, the American buttonwood, and the Scots pines of Europe all have distinct natural styles that are echoed in their bonsai forms, and particular horticultural idiosyncrasies that required the development of appropriate new techniques. Local clubs are formed by groups of enthusiasts, eager to help each other learn. Each year there are many local, national, and international conventions and seminars where amateurs and professionals gather to exhibit their trees and to increase their knowledge.

For centuries potted trees, like the flowering apricots pictured here, have been used in China to greet visitors to family residences and important buildings

Commercial bonsai

For most of us bonsai is not a quest for artistic fulfillment or a scientific challenge; it is simply a rewarding and creative pastime.

Our first encounter with bonsai was probably in a local garden center or department store, where modest little trees are sold for not-so-modest prices. Sadly, the high price seldom reflects a tree's artistic merit, but is due more to the fact that producing a bonsai is a time-consuming and labor-intensive operation, and then the plant has to be shipped halfway around the world!

Indoor bonsai

Ironically, although it was the Japanese who introduced bonsai to the West and first opened up the market here, the majority of commercial bonsai sold in the West today is produced in China. For one thing, there is no shortage of labor or space in China. But more importantly, the Chinese traditionally use sub-tropical or tropical species which, in temperate climates, need extra protection during winter. Furthermore, unlike hardy species, they can be kept indoors all year round if

need be, making them ideally suited to apartment-dwellers, and this way their appeal is broadened to the non-gardener.

The Chinese were very quick to seize the opportunity to exploit the West's growing fascination with bonsai, and set up large-scale nurseries to produce vast quantities of relatively cheap trees. At this low end of the range the plants are little more than two- or three-year-old rooted cuttings that have been hard-pruned once to induce a mass of new shoots prior to export. One person can prune up to a thousand plants in a day.

Medium-priced Chinese bonsai may often feature a clay figure or pagoda glued to a stone somewhere in the pot, but this is just the producer's idea of what appeals to westerners and should be discarded if not to your taste. The trees themselves, however, will have much more to offer. They are older, probably field-grown plants that have been hard-pruned. The new growth is shaped with wire or ties and allowed to grow for a season before being pruned again. Then they are regularly trimmed for another year or more before eventually being potted and ready for export.

A typical Japanese bonsai nursery, where plants are meticulously cared for and kept in perfect health

As the trees increase in price the true Chinese styles begin to emerge, and the more expensive specimens are likely to be truly authentic and full of Chinese magic. These are invariably collected from the wild, and can be extremely old. They are styled and refined for a number of years before being offered to overseas buyers. But even at this level, the Chinese make little effort to disguise the evidence of the hand of man. Saw cuts and pruned branches are allowed either to heal or to decay at nature's whim. It's as if the human intervention is just another episode of the tree's natural history.

Other far-eastern countries such as Taiwan and Korea are beginning to take large shares of the "indoor" bonsai market, concentrating on the low- to medium-priced trees – older, specimen bonsai from these sources are rare. Mediterranean countries such as Italy and Israel also produce small sub-tropical bonsai, mostly olives, pistachio, pomegranate, and the like. These can be a source of interesting material on which to work but, size for size, rarely have the charm or character of Far-Eastern trees.

Outdoor bonsai

In spite of indoor bonsai's more popular appeal, once hooked, the bonsai enthusiast invariably turns to hardy species. A collection of hardy bonsai, living in the open, rewards its owner with all the changes in color and texture associated with the seasons. Your work schedule will also be dictated by the seasons, each tree telling you when the time is right. As outdoor bonsai mature, the bark develops fissures and the soil becomes covered in moss. Outdoor bonsai bring you closer to nature and introduce greater challenges

and more possibilities, which is why they are preferred by the connoisseur.

Almost all hardy bonsai are produced in Japan. Generally, they are field-grown for between five and twenty years, sometimes even longer, but nowadays rarely collected from the wild; those that are tend to remain in Japan. While in the open ground, the trees receive some pruning and shaping before being lifted and examined. The trees

Right:
Thousands of *Acer palmatum* **starter trees under protection in a Japanese nursery**

Below:
Driftwood-style bonsai created from wild plants collected from the mountains. These are becoming increasingly rare and are now very expensive

with the most potential or with the fewest imperfections are retained for further development and the rest are exported as cheap "starter" trees.

The cycle is repeated, and each time the best are retained and the rest are exported at an appropriately higher price than the last batch. And at each successive cycle the standard of workmanship and the time taken over aesthetic consideration is increased. The essence of Japanese bonsai is the quest for perfection, and this system serves to maximize the artistic as well as the commercial potential of each particular tree.

Buying a bonsai

Bonsai are traditionally expensive, largely because they have to travel half-way around the world to reach you. Because of the high cost, you should understand what you are buying, and make sure you get the best deal.

Buying a bonsai

Your first introduction to bonsai might have been when you received one as a gift. If so, you're not alone. Almost half of all the imported tropical and sub-tropical bonsai are bought as gifts. On the other hand, you may have seen bonsai on display and decided you wanted to try keeping your own. Either way, the fact that you are reading this book indicates that you are interested enough to learn more, and to acquire more bonsai.

High Street bonsai
Bonsai have a reputation of being expensive which, as we saw in Chapter One, is often true. But you may not always get what you think you are paying for. Just before Christmas, so-called "bonsai" crop up everywhere – street markets, mall kiosks, garage sales, even flea markets, and you should beware of all of these. Some such traders will, no doubt, offer good-quality products at a reasonable price, but they are a minority. Shop around and compare prices and general health. Bear in mind that prices will fall in the January sales.

Japanese bonsai properly displayed in a nursery, each tree receiving adequate light and air to keep it healthy

Department stores also stock up with a number of indoor bonsai just before the Christmas rush. The better ones will offer trees recently imported from the far east. They will have spent weeks in a dark container, then in a heated greenhouse before winding up on the shelf. Most will be tough enough to recover if properly cared for, but generally in-store care is poor. Stores with a keener eye for an easy buck might offer tiny, recently rooted cuttings, in shallow pots, packed in boxes with clear windows. This keeps the plant green for a while, but the lack of light and fresh air weakens it tremendously. It is best not to buy these at all. If you

do, you will be paying for the packaging which, if the plant is to survive, must be discarded immediately.

Mail order
Many specialty nurseries offer a mail-order service. They pack the trees well and generally use contract carriers for next-day delivery. If you are unable to get to a specialty nursery and you are happy buying a bonsai without seeing it, then mail order is worth a try. Check first whether or not the supplier offers a refund for trees damaged on arrival, and unpack the tree while the delivery service is still at the door.

Advertisements in consumer magazines for mail-order bonsai should always be regarded with the utmost suspicion.

Specialty nurseries

There is no doubt that specialty nurseries are far and away the best places to buy bonsai. They depend on year-round business and rely heavily on repeat customers, so they have to be good. Most are run by people who became hooked on bonsai and turned their hobby into a business. As such, they have a good knowledge of bonsai care which they are always happy to pass on. They also stock all the bonsai paraphernalia such as training wire, tools, pots, fertilizers, and so on. Many will offer holiday care and "hospital" facilities for sick trees. They may also offer a repotting and pruning service, but after reading this book you shouldn't need either!

Wherever you decide to buy your bonsai, you should first arm yourself with a little knowledge to enable you to choose a good buy.

Health

Bonsai spend weeks in a shipping container and six months in quarantine before being offered for sale. By the time they reach the point of sale they should be in perfect condition. But, unlike plants in garden nurseries, bonsai can spend many months, or even years, waiting to be bought. With the best will in the world, some will inevitably contract various ailments or suffer from an unintentional lack of attention from time to time. Always check trees from the bottom upward.

Gently try to rock the trunk to see if the tree is secure in its pot. If it rocks easily, the roots are not completely filling the pot for some reason. This may mean that they are rotting or, at least, not growing well. Check that the drainage holes are adequate and are not blocked with roots. The presence of moss on the soil is a good sign, but water-loving plants such as liverwort indicate poor soil conditions.

• Look for old wounds which were not sealed properly and may be decaying. This can be difficult to arrest and may eventually cause more serious problems.

• Dead shoots may be a normal reaction to the lack of light and air caused by congested foliage. In these

Tropical bonsai need to be kept in an artificial environment – in the nursery and in the home. Here the conditions are ideal for the health and vigor of the plants

cases there is absolutely nothing to worry about because the shoots will readily regenerate once the tree receives your attention. Dead branches, though, are another matter. The loss of a branch may be caused by wire constriction, disease, root ailments, or mistreatment.

• Yellowing leaves can mean over- or underwatering, insufficient light, or a deficiency of trace elements, particularly magnesium. All of these are easily cured, but that should be the nursery's responsibility, not yours. Yellow leaves may also indicate more serious root problems, so try the trunk-rocking test.

• Dry areas of foliage can be caused by temporary conditions such as drafts or drought. This may also be caused by infestations of spider mites. In either case, if the leaves have totally withered, the likelihood is that the shoots have done likewise, perhaps even the entire branch.

• Finally, check the foliage for pests and evidence of fungal disease. Distorted or discolored leaves are normally caused by one or the other. Fortunately, most are easily cured, but once again, this should be the nursery's job.

Shape

The most important thing is that you find the shape of your bonsai pleasing, but don't be fooled by a dense canopy of bright green leaves. Trees have an internal structure of trunk and branches that also needs to be examined. The standard of workmanship that has gone into shaping the tree will also affect its quality. As with the health check, start at the bottom.

• On outdoor bonsai, the roots should be evenly distributed around the trunk and should flair naturally as they enter the soil. Twisted, crossing, or uneven visible roots are particularly ugly and generally impossible to rectify. On indoor trees, which follow the Chinese style, the roots are normally

intentionally exposed and randomly arranged. Here the emphasis is on the bizarre, but they should still appear natural.

• Many desirable varieties are grafted onto root stocks of a similar variety. Graft unions almost always leave a permanent scar and often swell, disfiguring the trunk. Poor graft unions get worse as time passes, not better. Japanese white pine (*Pinus parviflora*) are always grafted onto black pine (*Pinus thunbergii*) root stocks. The union is made just below the first branch to take advantage of the black

Above: Beware of poor grafts, especially on maples. The swelling will get worse as time passes

Left: A tangled root mass like this is inefficient and will require reorganizing if the plant is to progress

pine's fissured bark. Normally the first branch is trained to hide the graft union, so make sure this branch is healthy and does its job properly.

• Trunks have an infinite variety of shapes – on indoor trees they may be coiled or dramatically bent back on themselves. On outdoor trees they are more likely to follow conventional tree-like forms. In either case, the trunk should taper from base to apex and should be clear of branches for about the bottom third. It should also be completely free of ugly scars. With group or forest plantings, the trunks should be varied in height, thickness, and spacing, and no one trunk should obscure another.

• Mass-produced bonsai are wire-trained just like any other, and are often

exported with the wire still on. This is not a problem in itself, but it is not uncommon to find that the wire has already begun to cut into the bark, causing spiral scars that will take many years to heal. Occasionally you may find bonsai with wire deeply embedded in the bark and impossible to remove. Don't believe the myth that this is done to artificially "age" the tree. It is the result of carelessness and nothing else.

• All bonsai are hard-pruned at some point in their preparation for sale, and all pruning will leave a scar of some sort. When working on your own trees, carefully hollow out the wound and seal it (*see Chapter Seven*). However, this is not practical on a

commercial scale, so short stubs are left which can be cut off and hollowed out when you get the tree home. Before you buy, consider how this could be done. A trunk that has been cut through at right angles to reduce height and induce branching will not only have an unnatural shape, but the large scar will be a permanent feature. A good bonsai should either show no scars at all or should have all pruning wounds incorporated into the design, by carving them into natural-looking hollows or shaping and bleaching the stubs to create jins (*see Chapter Seven*).

• The easiest way to learn how to assess the branch structure of a bonsai is to look at the full-size trees around you. On old conifers the branches are horizontal or sweep downward and each bears wide shallow pads of foliage. The branches become progressively shorter and thinner as they grow higher up the trunk, giving the tree a conical shape. On deciduous trees branches are horizontal or sweep gently upward, frequently forking. Each branch bears a mass of foliage which forms part of the overall dome-shaped canopy. Branches are distributed evenly around the trunk. Making allowances for scale and the desire for an "interesting" shape, the same principle applies to bonsai, albeit in a simpli-

Right: Wire scars on branches or trunks weakens the tree and will take many years to heal

Below: Trident maples readily form a strong buttress at the base of the trunk, much prized in Japan

fied way. Check for wire marks and ugly pruning scars. Also, avoid trees with two branches positioned immediately opposite each other. These "bar branches" will jar the eye

and in the future will cause the trunk to swell where they join it.

Species

Before buying a bonsai you must consider where it will be expected to live. If you want a tree for indoors, assess the light and temperature levels in the room, and decide whether or not you can put the tree outside during summer. If you prefer outdoor bonsai, you need to consider the amount of sunlight your garden receives. Can you provide dappled shade all day or protection from the hot afternoon sun? The following pages provide a guide to the species which are suitable for various home environments.

Bright sunny rooms

Many modern homes have large picture windows which admit plenty of light. South- or west-facing windows will also admit hot sun whose effect is amplified by the glass. Many species will suffer in these conditions, and should be kept away from the direct sun, but close enough to the window to receive good light. Don't keep your trees on the window sill because at night the temperature close to the glass can fall dramatically, particularly in winter when the central heating is off. This constant extreme temperature fluctuation can be fatal to tropical and sub-tropical bonsai. Positioning trees some distance from the window will reduce the strength of the sunlight and broaden the range of species you can   successfully grow.

Right: Podocarpus love bright, warm conditions

Right: Podocarpus love bright, warm conditions and will thrive close to a large, sunny window in a centrally heated apartment

Suitable species
• Bamboos
• Bougainvillaea
• Lagerstroemia
• Ligustrum
• Murraya
• Olive
• *Punica granatum*
• Pistachio
• Podocarpus
• Serrissa
• *Ulmus parvifolia*

receive adequate light. The lights generate slight heat which can also benefit the trees, but the drying effect of this needs to be countered by regular spraying and extra vigilance when watering.

Suitable species
- Carmona
- Cycas
- Ficus
- Myrtus
- Nandina
- Sageretia

Dark rooms

North or east-facing rooms may appear quite dark, but close to the window there will be sufficient light to keep several species perfectly happy.

One solution to the problem of low natural light is to install specially made artificial lighting for your bonsai collection. This is not as costly or impractical as it might at first seem. Although there are a number of horticul-

tural lighting systems on the market, ordinary, blue-white fluorescent strip lighting provides the complete spectrum of light needed by most species, and is cheap to run. The drawback is that their light is fairly low-intensity. Ideally, the strips should be positioned between 8 and 12 in. (200 and 300 mm) from the foliage. Use three strips, positioning two directly above the trees – one toward the front and another further back – and the third lower down, behind the trees. Keep the lights on for seven to ten hours a day and rotate the trees 90 degrees every few days to ensure that all parts

Above Right: Extra light can be provided by placing two or three fluorescent strip lights directly above the trees

Right: Ficus are tough plants that are accustomed to the shadier, more humid conditions below taller trees

Sunny gardens

In mid-summer, the heat from the after-noon sun is reflected off fences, buildings, and patios, sending the local temperature soaring. Pots heat up and dry out rapidly. The sunlight is intense and can itself be damaging, particularly in recent years, when its harmful rays are not so efficiently filtered by the atmosphere. Some species, especially when grown in pots, dislike such intense, hot sun – others positively love it. But all bonsai should have their pots shaded or regularly cooled with water during very hot spells in order to prevent the roots from becoming too hot and cooking. Erecting a special-built shaded area will enable you to grow a wider range of species.

Right: Chinese junipers are adapted to life on exposed mountains where they receive full sun. Providing similar conditions in your garden will keep the foliage compact

Suitable species
• Celtis
• Chaenomeles
• Chinese juniper
• Cotoneaster
• Cryptomeria
• *Ilex crenata*
• Needle juniper
• Malus
• Picea
• White pine
• Black pine
• Pyracantha
• Ulmus
• Wisteria

Shaded gardens

In many ways a shaded garden provides the ideal environment for bonsai, provided the sky directly above your bonsai is not obscured by overhanging trees and the sun is reflected off a wall or fence into the garden for at least part of the day to maintain seasonal temperatures. Even species that prefer full sun will do quite nicely with good overhead light, although the growth might be a little "leggy." This can be controlled by reducing the nitrogen in the feeding program, and regular trimming.

Right: The foliage, flowers and colored bark of Stewartia all perform best in shadier conditions

Suitable species
- Azaleas
- Japanese maples
- Trident maple
- Hornbeams
- Ginkgo
- Yew
- Chamaecyparis
- Beech
- Stewartia
- Zelkova

How a tree works

It is easy enough to carry out the instructions that follow regarding watering, feeding, and pruning, but understanding a little about how a tree functions will increase your enjoyment of bonsai and give you more confidence in caring for your trees.

Roots

Because the roots are out of sight, it is very easy to overlook the importance of a healthy, vigorous root system. More often than not, when a bonsai begins to look sickly it is an indication of some form of root disorder.

Roots have three functions. First, they provide anchorage, holding the tree firm in the ground. In the wild they do this by growing in all directions and eventually thickening to form a buttress at the base of the trunk. Second, they absorb moisture and soluble nutrients from the soil. Third, they store sugars during dormancy, to provide energy for the first flush of growth in spring. Let's look at these functions in more detail.

Anchorage

This may seem rather irrelevant to bonsai but in fact the roots are still responsible for holding the tree firm in the pot. You will see in the section on repotting (see page 48) that wire can be used to hold the tree firm initially, but this is unsightly and is therefore only temporary. If the roots lack vigor or are decaying, they will not fill the pot and the trunk will rock in the wind or as you work on the tree. This causes further damage to the roots, and so the vicious circle continues.

Left: The plump, white growing tips indicate a healthy and vigorous root system

To hold a tree firmly in its pot, the roots must be distributed all around the trunk and must grow sideways rather than downward. One-sided root systems are unstable and will most likely also result in a one-sided branch structure. Roots that grow steeply downward before spreading sideways tend to rely more on fine roots to provide anchorage.

Absorbing water and nutrients

Healthy, growing roots show plump and white at the tips. This is the most active part of the root system. The very tip is protected as it thrusts its way through the soil by a hard cap which is constantly being worn away and replaced. Behind this, the white part of the root is clothed in minute root hairs, which are composed of a single cell and can be almost invisible to the naked eye. Although water can be absorbed by older parts of the root, it is through these root hairs that the water and, most importantly, nutrients are more readily absorbed due to their enormous com-

bined surface area. Root hair production is stimulated by moisture and oxygen present in the soil.

Absorption of water takes place by the process of osmosis. The membranes surrounding root cells are semi-permeable – which means they have millions of tiny pores just big enough to allow one water molecule to pass through. When the concentration of nutrient salts inside the root is greater than immediately outside, water molecules pass through the pores into the root hairs to dilute the solution. This means that the solution of salts in the root hairs is now weaker than in the adjacent cell, so water molecules pass one cell further into the root, and so on. Once the water has reached the xylem cells in the core of the root it is drawn up the tree by capillary action.

The pores in the semi-permeable membrane are big enough to allow water molecules to pass, but not dissolved nutrients. They are absorbed electrochemically. All the chemicals in question are either positively or negatively charged. When the tree requires a particular nutrient – say, potash – which is positively charged, the root expels a positively charged hydrogen ion to make way for it. Simultaneously, one pore changes size and shape to allow just one potassium ion through into the root.

Nobody is sure how the tree can judge its nutrient requirements so precisely, but this remarkable micro-scopic process takes place hundreds of millions of times a day.

Root burn

If the concentration of salts outside the roots is greater than that inside, the osmosis is reversed and water passes out of the roots back into the soil to equalize the solutions. The tree will wilt and begin to shed young shoots. This is why you should never use fertilizers in excess of the recommended rates or when the roots are inactive. Similarly, feeding directly after repotting, when there are few, if any, root hairs, can have a similar effect. Regular prolonged watering to flush the soil clean of residual salts is a wise precaution.

Nutrient storage

Older, thicker roots develop bundles of sap-conducting cells called the phloem, which is also present in the trunk and branches. These cells conduct the sugars from the leaves and distribute them to all parts of the plant,

Above: The spreading roots on this azalea look like fingers grasping the soil. This type of root structure is efficient as well as imparting strength and character to the tree

wherever they are needed for growth, including to the roots. In late summer and autumn, when growth slows down and eventually ceases, the phloem becomes plump with excess sugars which are stored there until they are needed to support new growth in spring. Transplanting trees and pruning roots in autumn causes considerable loss of stored sugars, which will retard spring growth. This is why you should wait until the buds begin to swell, which indicates that at least some of the stored sugars have been returned to the growing points, before pruning the roots. The exceptions are some flowering plants which seem to produce even more flowers and fruit if given a hard time and repotted in autumn.

Trunks and branches

The main purpose of the trunk and branches of a tree is purely structural, i.e., to support as much foliage as possible in positions where it will receive the most light and air. They also, naturally, have to conduct water, nutrients and sugars from roots to leaves and back. In a mature tree most of the tissue forming the trunk and branches – the heartwood – is dead. It has become lignified (literally, turned into wood) and hardened, and is responsible for the tree's strength. Naturally, the thicker the heartwood, the more difficult it is to bend. The actual living part of the trunk and branches is confined to the outermost layers, and it is here that all the activity takes place .

The cambium

If you gently scratch a twig with your fingernail you will notice a bright green layer just below the surface. This is the cambium, a single layer of cells surrounding the trunk, branches and shoots. The cambium is constantly developing new cells of different types, both on the inside and the outside, throughout the growing season. It also has the ability to initiate new buds or new roots, and to fuse with the cambium of another plant, such as when grafting.

When a thick branch is cut through during the growing season, the cambium has a heyday. It responds to the loss of a branch by generating a mass of completely new shoots which emerge like a crown from between the bark and the sapwood in an attempt to replace the lost foliage. Most of these shoots will die off through overcrowding and lack of light, but the strongest will continue to grow vigorously.

The cambium is also responsible for producing the healing tissue that rolls over wounds. If you look closely at a recent pruning cut, you can see how this tissue emerges from between the bark and the wood.

The xylem

On the inside of the cambium the new cells it produces form the xylem, which conducts the water upward. It is the formation of new xylem each year that creates the familiar annual rings. The xylem remains active for a year or more, depending on the species, and while active, forms what is referred to as sapwood. This is the lighter-colored group of rings surrounding the heartwood. The rate of a tree's growth and the pattern of its xylem cells determine the strength and grain of its wood.

The production of new xylem is also what makes branches set in position when trained with wire. Once the tensile strength of the new xylem is sufficient to counter that of the old wood, the wire may be removed and the branch will stay in place. The wood in young shoots and

Above: Deciduous trees such as maples reward you with year-round interest as they change in response to the seasons

Right: The broad, spreading foliage pads of this Cedar of Lebanon are typical of ancient conifers and provide inspiration for the bonsai artist

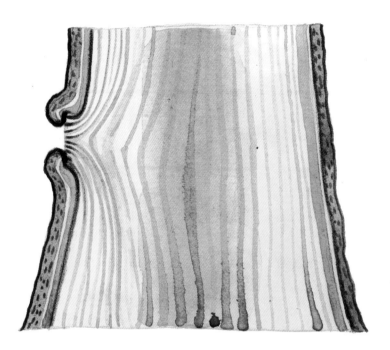

branchlets is composed entirely of xylem which is malleable and will readily adopt new shapes. Older branches that contain heartwood take longer to set. The tensions created by bending the branch will always be present, and even if a branch appears to have set, it may gradually move back toward its original position as the soft xylem yields under pressure from the tough heartwood.

The phloem

On the outside of the cambium the new cells form the phloem, which distributes the sugars manufactured by the leaves to all other parts of the plant. As old phloem cells are replaced by new ones each year, they in turn harden and become the bark. As the years pass the bark thickens, and in most cases becomes corky and flakes, peels or develops fissures. The precise formation of phloem cells and the length of their useful lives differs between one species and another. This explains why different trees display their own unique characteristic bark patterns as they mature.

Why bonsai live so long

In the wild, a healthy tree will continue growing until it reaches its genetically predetermined

Above: Each year a new layer of wood is formed which gradually "rolls" over wounds until they are completely healed

Above right: When thick branches are pruned, masses of new shoots emerge from the cambium layer between the bark and the sapwood. Most of these will die off through overcrowding, and only the strongest will continue to grow

height. Once this has been achieved the crown begins to spread sideways, generally forming a dome. Eventually, the distance between the active roots at the periphery of the root system and the increasing mass of foliage at the tips of the branches become too great and the tree begins to deteriorate. As the foliage receives less water and nutrients from the roots it is therefore less able to supply adequate sugars to generate new roots and the tree eventually dies.

Trees that are regularly pruned, such as those that are pollarded, or hedgerow trees, live for much longer than their full-size counterparts because they never

reach their maximum dimensions. They will not die of old age until the structural heartwood rots and collapses.

Because a bonsai is constantly being encouraged, by pruning, to produce new healthy roots and shoots, it is always actively growing, trying to reach maturity. The actual living part – the cambium, flanked by the xylem and the phloem – is never more than a few years old. Provided enough growth takes place each year to lay down sufficient new xylem and phloem to sustain the tree, a bonsai will always remain essentially young and should, in theory at least, live forever.

Leaves

Each leaf is a highly efficient food factory that converts water from the soil and carbon dioxide from the air into essential sugars in a process called photosynthesis. As this term implies, light – normally sunlight – is an important catalyst in this process. Without sufficient light the leaves lose much of their green chlorophyll, the substance that enables photosynthesis to take place, consequently losing their ability to function.

Some shade is preferable for almost all plants grown in containers, but deep shade will cause problems, as will excessive sun. Too much sun, although providing the necessary light, will cause the leaves to overheat. They will rapidly close their breathing pores (stomata) in order to reduce water evaporation. This effectively causes the leaf to "shut down" until the sun becomes less intense. During this time the leaf is not manufacturing sugars because the process relies on a constant passage of water through the leaf, and also a constant supply of carbon dioxide, which is absorbed through the same stomata. Precisely how much sun is too much depends entirely on the species.

Leaf types

Plants that normally live in semi-shade, such as azaleas and Japanese maples, have delicate, thin-skinned leaves which will easily become brown and withered at the edges if grown in full sun or if exposed to drying winds. At the other end of the scale, plants which normally live exposed to the hot sun have thick, leathery leaves, often with a waxy coating which helps prevent water evaporation. A similar waxy coating is also used by some species that prefer extremely cold conditions. Most conifers have waxy leaves, but this time the idea is essentially to protect them from the cold, and also to help prevent snow and frost from adhering to the needles.

The variety of leaf color and shape is endless. This variety is what makes collecting different species so fascinating. The size can also vary considerably, not only between species, but also even within the same variety, depending on the growing conditions of the individual plant. Plants growing in the ground or in large containers in semi-shade will bear large, deep-green leaves. The same variety growing in a small bonsai pot in full sun will have much smaller leaves which will not display the same richness of color.

A waxy coating conserves water and protects against freezing

Following stress, the foliage becomes more open for a season or two

Above: No waxy coating is necessary
Below: A thick waxy coating protects against severe cold or hot sun

Buds

On most species there is a tiny, embryonic bud at the base of each leaf stalk (petiole). Take a plump savoy cabbage and slice it in half and you will see a greatly magnified version of a typical bud – for that is precisely what a cabbage is. You will also be able to see the smaller buds at the bases of the petioles. Reduce this cabbage to 0.5 mm across and you have a typical bud on, for example, a Chinese elm. As the bud opens in spring, the central core elongates to form at the shoot with leaves distributed at intervals (internodes) along its length. As it extends, the bud at the growing tip is constantly undergoing a cycle of opening, extension, and regeneration. If this is removed the energy will be diverted into the next one or two buds back down the shoot.

Each bud is surrounded by scales which can be anything from green, through browns, to bright red, depending on the species. The scales are designed to protect the delicate partly formed leaves in the bud from the sun, rain, frost, and insect attack. They are, in fact, modified leaves and, as such, also have embryonic buds at the base of each scale. This explains why a mass of new shoots emerges from the short stub left when hard-pruning the current year's growth.

Buds can also be formed on old wood in reaction to more severe pruning or to some other trauma. The cambium layer *(see page 34, trunks & branches)* works to regenerate lost foliage by rapidly developing new buds which force their way through the bark. These are called adventitious buds and can appear on branches, trunks, and even on old roots near the surface of the soil. When you see a tree in the countryside that has lots of adventitious buds on its trunk and branches, you can be sure that it has recently suffered some kind of trauma – either drought, physical damage, or perhaps a severe attack of some fungal disease or insect pest. In bonsai cultivation the production of adventitious buds is of key importance because they are selectively used to grow new shoots to replace outgrown or congested areas of foliage.

Buds are a useful indicator of the state of a tree's growth in spring. As the tree begins to stir from its dormancy, the buds start to swell. Tiny paler-colored lines will be seen at the edge of each scale as they begin to separate. This indicates an increase in root activity and tells us to get on with the repotting before growth is too far advanced.

Autumn color

One of the most charming and rewarding aspects of trees, large or small, is the vivid autumn coloration, which can vary from bright yellow through reds to purple. Many of these colored pigments are in the leaves from the time the shoots emerge from the buds, but are masked by the presence of chlorophyll. In red-leaved maples the pigments exist in greater quantity than the chlorophyll, so the masking effect is reversed. Grow a red-leaved maple in deep shade and it will produce more chlorophyll and turn green. If kept in a brighter position the leaves may stay red all summer. Other pigments are the result of chemical changes that take place in early autumn. As autumn approaches the leaves cease producing sugars and the chlorophyll breaks down and, along with other minerals, is re-absorbed by the plant.

Autumn color can be enhanced by keeping your trees in a warm, sunny spot during the day in late summer and early autumn, but keeping them as cold as possible at night. This ensures that the color-forming breakdown of substances continues at its maximum rate during the day, but their redistribution to other parts of the plant is hindered by the night-time cold.

Don't worry if your bonsai lose their leaves before full-sized trees lose theirs. This is quite common and, although disappointing, does no harm.

Below right: This magnified bud reveals a tightly compressed mass of embryonic leaves, complete with stem and another terminal bud

Below left: The upper surface of a leaf absorbs sunlight which helps convert water and carbon dioxide into nourishing sugars. The underside contains the pores – stomata – through which the plant breathes

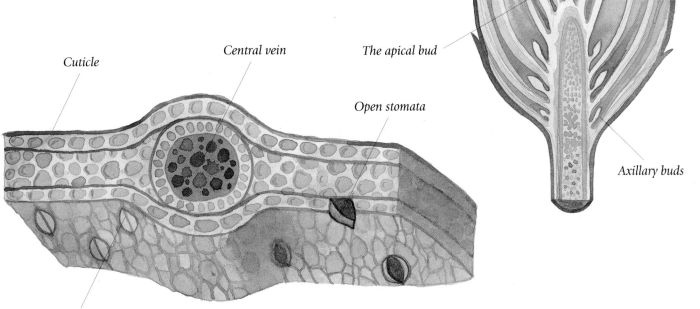

Bud scales

The apical bud

Axillary buds

Cuticle

Central vein

Open stomata

Closed stomata

Light, water, and air

All plants need an adequate supply of light, water, and air, but there is a world of difference between sunlight and sunshine, between moist and waterlogged soil, or between fresh air and a draft.

Left: Delicate leaves, such as those on Japanese maples, are easily "scorched" if exposed to drying winds

Light

As we saw in Chapter Three, leaves need a certain amount of sunlight in order to photosynthesize and nourish the plant with sugars. In too shady conditions leaves will grow larger to gather as much light as possible; the internodes (distances between leaves) will increase as the plant rapidly tries to extend shoots to reach through the overhead canopy to the sun. In good light, leaves will be smaller and internodes much shorter. If the sun is too strong, many plants will throw out new growth from close to the trunk, where it is shaded by the scorched outer foliage. Many plants also use day length, rather than temperature, to trigger seasonal phases such as flowering or leaf-fall.

Bearing in mind, of course, that different species prefer different amounts of sunlight, it is important to learn a little about the natural habitat of the full-size cousins of your bonsai. Pines and junipers that are found growing on exposed mountain sides are naturally adapted to tolerate full sun. Indeed, growth can be rather disappointing when grown in shady conditions. A bonsai pine or juniper, when kept close to a wall, will grow vigorously on the open side but may even start to die back on the shaded side.

On the other hand, if you keep a maple or an azalea, both plants of woodland margins and valleys, in an exposed situation, the side away from the sun will produce much healthier and more vigorous growth. The leaves of red maples will hold their color for longer if kept in semi-shade, although returning them to full sun in autumn will greatly intensify seasonal color.

Right: Insufficient light causes the shoots to become leggy and the internodes (spaces between the leaves) to extend out of proportion to the tree

In bonsai we try to strike a happy medium. Few people can provide perfect conditions for all species, but most can find a sunny corner or erect some shade netting. Your bonsai isn't going to die through too much or too little sunlight – but it will tell you that it's not happy.

One final point. Remember to turn each bonsai 90 degrees every few days, so that each area of foliage receives an equal amount of light.

Water

Surprisingly, more bonsai – or any other type of potted plant – are lost through overwatering than through drought. Very few species can tolerate permanently saturated soil and

Left: Colored foliage can become green if light levels are too low. The upper leaves here remain red while those they are shading are beginning to turn green

Some species – known as calcifuges – do not tolerate lime, which may cause problems in areas where the tapwater is "hard," or rich in lime. Using an acid, organic-based soil and giving regular applications of a proprietary soil-acidifier will counteract hard water. In extreme cases, exposed roots may become encrusted with lime deposit, which is harmless but unsightly. This can be removed with a stiff toothbrush. Never use artificially "softened" water. Water softeners replace the calcium with sodium, which is even worse.

Tapwater contains all sorts of added chemicals which are designed to "purify" it, or to strengthen our teeth, and so on. None of these chemicals are particularly harmful to plants in low concentrations. However, occasionally higher-than-normal quantities of chlorine are introduced, particularly when water supplies are low or are drawn from rivers, and the weather is warm. If you allow the water to stand in an open container for a few hours before use the chlorine will evaporate.

Allowing the water to stand also brings it to the ambient temperature. Applying ice-cold water to a sun-warmed pot can shock the root system and cause temporary damage

some prefer dry roots for part of the year (*for details of these see the Tree Directory*). But most require soil that remains moist at the driest and is never allowed to dry out completely between waterings.

If you are not sure whether your trees need watering, gently scratch away the surface of the soil to see how damp it is underneath. If it is just damp, then you can apply water; if it is wet, then leave it alone. If the soil is bone dry, water immediately using the immersion technique described below. After a while, you should be able to judge how wet the soil is simply by the weight of the pot.

Water quality
Without doubt, rainwater is by far the best for all plants, even in these days of acid rain. However, it is not always possible to collect sufficient rainwater to last more than a week or so in the summer. Storing large quantities of water for a long time has its dangers too. Air-borne spores of fungi such as phytopthera can enter the tank and, when watered into the pot, will attack the roots of your bonsai. Always keep water barrels tightly closed, and flush them out with disinfectant and clean tap water at regular intervals.

Right: Poorly drained soil will rapidly compact and become waterlogged. In soil like this the roots cannot breathe and will soon begin to rot

to the delicate growing tips. On the other hand, water that is a few degrees cooler than the roots will refresh them and cool them down on hot days. The trick is to water either in the early morning or in the evening, when the roots are not so over-heated. If you have a large collection of bonsai, you may choose to use a hose with a fine spray attachment for watering. Remember: if a hose is left lying in the sun all day the water in it will become very hot indeed. Always let the water run for a few minutes before using it on your trees.

Overhead watering

Obviously, the most natural way for a plant to receive water is from above. If your bonsai are properly potted – with the free-draining soil level just below the rim of the pot – this method should never cause a problem. However, there are a few points to watch.

• Use a fine-spray attachment on your hose or watering can. Excessive force will wash away the surface soil and tend to compact the rest.

• Fill the space between the surface of the soil and the rim of the pot with water and allow it to completely soak in. Then repeat the process. By this time water should be emerging from the drainage holes in the pot.

• If no water emerges from the drainage holes after two applications, it might mean that the soil is too compact or in poor condition, or perhaps the drainage holes are blocked. Unblock the drainage holes and, in the future, use the immersion watering technique described below until you repot the tree at the earliest appropriate time.

• Make sure you water the entire surface of the soil. The area behind the trunk is frequently neglected when watering in a hurry, and this can weaken the roots in that area as well as the branches directly above them.

• Avoid the temptation to give all your bonsai the same amount of water every day. Watering *en masse* is all right for a limited period in summer, but check the pots individually every few days and adjust the watering as necessary.

• Don't water in full sun unless the water has been allowed to stand for an hour or two.

• The leaves will enjoy being wetted at watering time provided that they are not in full sun at the time. If you are using foliar plant foods, or if the water is particularly hard, powdery deposits may appear on

the foliage. This will normally wash off when it rains.

Immersion watering

When bonsai trees are pot-bound the roots become so dense that water is very slow to penetrate. You may see water running from the drainage holes, but this may have merely trickled between the soil and the pot, without wetting the soil at all.

Imported indoor bonsai are generally planted in dense clay-like soils which may be fine in the growing nursery but are not appropriate for long-term use in domestic conditions. The soil becomes very compacted and is reluctant to absorb water. Furthermore,

the soil is frequently mounded up above the rim of the pot so that the water just runs off before it has had a chance to soak in. In conditions like these, the immersion technique can get you and your bonsai out of trouble.

The immersion technique for watering bonsai: place the bonsai in a bowl or bath and slowly add water until it covers the surface of the soil entirely. You should see bubbles rising from the soil as the water replaces the air in the soil. If no bubbles appear, it may be because

Below: Immersion watering. Immersing the entire pot in water every so often drives out all the stale air and ensures that there are no persistent dry spots. When the bubbles stop rising, the pot can be removed from the water and drained

the soil is very compacted. Wait until the bubbles have stopped rising (or for half an hour if there were no bubbles) and then remove the pot from the water. Tilt the pot to drain off excess water. A number of enthusiasts who normally water from overhead immerse all their pots once a month to ensure that there are no hidden areas of dry roots.

Automatic watering

Many commercial plant nurseries use a variety of automatic watering systems ranging from overhead sprays to individual drip-feeds. These are fine if you want to maintain a large number of virtually identical plants, but not so reliable when each plant requires more individual attention. Some experienced bonsai growers use timed low-level sprays or drip feeds while they are away from home, but they need extremely careful planning. The best advice is not to use automatic systems at all.

Air

Like people, trees need fresh air in order to remain healthy. Poor air circulation, either around the leaves and branches or around the roots (see page 48), will result in poor, sickly growth and creates ideal conditions for fungal and bacterial spores to take hold. Indoor bonsai that spend their lives in centrally heated, smoke-filled rooms will suffer just as badly as humans. The only difference is that the effect will be much more pronounced. Inner shoots will wither, leaves will become covered in powdery mildew, insects will colonize the foliage, and the soil and trunk will become covered in algae.

To maintain good air circulation, indoors or outdoors, bonsai should be placed at about waist-height, preferably on their own stand indoors or on slatted benches outside. This allows air of ambient

Right: Yellowing leaves may seem to be caused by dry soil but, more often than not, they result from overwatering or drafts

Left: Automatic watering systems ensure that an even amount of water is supplied to every plant, but they take no account of each plant's individual needs

temperature to circulate freely around all parts of the tree. Indoors, if placed lower, the air will be cooler than room temperature; if placed higher it will be warmer – and drier. Outdoors, trees that are placed too low will not only be short-changed as far as fresh air is concerned, but they will also be prey to all the neighborhood snails, slugs, and, worst of all, cats!

However, it is important to recognize the difference between fresh air circulation and drafts. A draft is a fast-moving current, usually colder than the surrounding air. Its effect can be devastating, causing rapid yellowing and shedding of leaves and die-back of young shoots. The pot cools down rapidly, restricting root growth. Once you have found a situation that seems to suit your bonsai, leave it there.

Outdoors, wind can also be harmful to bonsai. Clearly, strong winds can tear at the foliage of any species, which not only disfigures the leaves but also reduces their efficiency. Even moderate winds can have a severe drying effect, which is as dangerous during winter as it is in summer. Species that are adapted to live in the relative protection of woodland margins or sheltered valleys, such as azaleas, Japanese maples, and hornbeams, will develop brown edges on the leaves if exposed to wind.

Life in a pot

When confined to a pot, a tree is unable to seek out sources of water or nutrients. It cannot grow faster to beat an infestation of pests, or to reach the sun. Its delicate roots and leaves can become bone-dry in a matter of hours, or can gradually suffocate in waterlogged soil. Your bonsai relies on you for its entire life-support.

Drainage

Ironically, your worst enemy is not drought, but root decay caused by overwatering or poor drainage. For this reason it is essential to use a soil that is *very* free-draining. When you water the soil, the water should not lie on the surface. It should pass directly through the soil and begin flowing from the drainage holes within half a minute or so. This type of soil also ensures that waterlogging does not occur even after prolonged rainfall. Remember, it is far easier to add water to soil than it is to remove it!

Water retention

As well as being free-draining, a soil must be able to hold sufficient water to satisfy the tree's needs until the next watering. A soil containing fine particles, such as most garden soil, would retain water but would soon become compacted and impede drainage. To prevent this, it is necessary to use larger particles of water-retaining material – either organic or mineral.

Air spaces

Roots also need to "breathe" in order to function efficiently, and the micro-organisms that help them digest nutrients also require oxygen. Compacted soil, or soil composed of particles that fit closely together, will not contain sufficient air spaces to maintain healthy roots. Under these conditions, the helpful bacteria will perish and damaging anaerobic bacteria, which promote root decay, will thrive.

What soil?

Japanese bonsai growers invariably use a commercial soil called "Akadama." It is a hard, coarse, clay-like soil that has a natural granular structure with particles ranging in size up to ¼ in. (1-6 mm). It holds water but has excellent drainage and contains ample air spaces. Even after several years' use the granular structure is retained. Although it can be fairly expensive in the West, experienced enthusiasts are increasingly turning to Akadama soil because of its unique properties, using it straight or mixing it with grit or sand for pines and drought-adapted species.

Proprietary potting composts are intended for houseplants growing in deep pots, which require far less fre-

Grit or sharp sand is a basic ingredient for a homemade bonsai soil

Japanese Akadama soil is perfect for most bonsai, but can be expensive

Organic matter (leaf mold or peat) is a basic ingredient for a homemade bonsai soil

quent watering and are not expected to live for as long as a bonsai. Moreover, most houseplants are perennials or, at most, sub-shrubs which are not as particular as trees. Commercial potting composts will rapidly compact and become waterlogged in shallow containers, and therefore should not be used unless properly sieved and mixed with grit or sand *(see below)*.

Many nurseries market their own "bonsai soils," which vary greatly in quality. They invariably use ingredients that are readily available to the amateur and are seldom prepared with as much care as you might take when preparing your own. This is not carelessness on the part of the nursery, but the time-consuming sifting-out of fine particles and the resulting waste is simply not cost-effective. These soils are all right for a short time but, to get the best from your bonsai, you should either use Akadama or mix your own soil so you can control the quality of the ingredients and the size of the particles.

Mixing your own soil

A good, reliable, basic bonsai soil consists of just two ingredients: organic matter and grit.

Water retention is provided by organic matter such as peat, leaf mold, composted bark, and so on. This should not be so far decomposed that it crumbles to dust easily when dry. Ideally, if moist organic matter is squeezed tightly in the hand, it should spring apart again when the pressure is released. Garden compost and farmyard manure are tempting, but they are too rich in nutrients for the delicate, freshly pruned roots, and often contain bacterial or fungal diseases. Whatever organic matter you choose, you can expect to discard at least 60 percent in the sifting process.

All lumps larger than ¼ in. (5 mm) should first be either broken up or removed. The remainder must then be scrupulously sifted to remove all particles smaller than 2 mm. Particles smaller than this will be washed to the base of the pot and impede drainage and aeration. Sift when the material is just damp. If wet, it will clog the mesh of the sieve. If dry, the action of sifting will cause some particles to crumble to dust and cause unnecessary waste.

An open, free-draining, and well-ventilated structure is ensured by the addition of grit or coarse sand. This must also be sifted to retain particles from 2-5 mm (or 2-3 mm in smaller pots). Use only prepared horticultural grit or sand. Under no circumstances should you use

fresh builders' sand. Builders' sand often contains natural or introduced impurities which can be extremely harmful to plants. If you have no alternative, buy the sand a year or two in advance, sift it, and leave it in the open so the rain can wash out the impurities.

River sand is best because the grains are rounded, so even when fully settled, they don't fit tightly together. This ensures ample drainage and air spaces. Crushed granite or flint is easier to obtain and will do the job well, but the grains have flat sides which can fit close together. To counter this, use a more stable organic material such as composted bark, rather than soft peat or leaf mold. Never use beach sand, which contains salt, oil, and other fatal impurities which are difficult to remove.

Finally, mix the two ingredients in roughly equal proportions. It is best to do this while the organic matter is still slightly damp – if it is wet it will not mix well, and if it is bone dry it will tend to break down to dust during the mixing process. Store unused soil in a sealed plastic sack to keep it damp.

For species that require a more free-draining soil, such as those that are adapted to live in mountains or dry areas, you can add more coarse grit *(see details in the Tree Directory)*. For added water retention, it is best to avoid the temptation to add more organic matter,

Both grit and organic matter (see opposite) are mixed in equal parts to form an open, water retentive but free drained soil

Proprietary soil improvers, such as this calcined clay or crushed pumice, can be added to the mix to ensure that it remains absorbent and free-draining for a long period. They can also be used alone if extra care can be taken when watering

but to reduce the aggregate particle size of the grit to 1-3 mm. Alternatively, you can replace some of the grit with one of the proprietary granular soil conditioners on the market.

Soil conditioners

In recent years a variety of soil conditioners have been developed for professional nurseries and gardeners. These include crushed pumice, baked or calcined clay, and various other mineral composites. They are all available in suitable particle sizes and have the advantage of retaining their structures indefinitely, and can be added to the basic mix in order to increase water retention without impeding drainage. Some growers have achieved considerable success by substituting all organic matter with pumice or calcined clay, controlling the amount of water retained by adjusting the proportion of grit, sometimes eliminating it entirely. In theory this is fine, but I have reservations about using totally inert soils. Plants need a "living" soil, and only organic matter can provide this.

Having prepared your basic mix you may have to adjust it, depending on the particular requirements of some species. Details of variations to the basic mix are given in the Tree Directory.

appropriate time. It is a good idea to keep watering to a minimum and to use only foliar feeds until this can be done.

The best time of year to prune the roots is in late winter to early spring, just as the buds begin to swell slightly. This indicates that the roots are also becoming active and will therefore regenerate rapidly. It is not possible to state a precise time for repotting; only close observation of the tree can tell you when the time is right, because

Repotting

We saw in Chapter Three how necessary it is to maintain a constant cycle of regenerating young, active roots in order to keep a bonsai healthy and long-lived. This is achieved by periodically repotting the tree and pruning the roots. This process may seem "cruel" to the uninitiated, but it is, in fact, highly beneficial to the tree if carried out properly.

When to repot

Detailed advice on the frequency of repotting for individual species is given in the Plant Index. But as a general rule, young or small bonsai require repotting every two or three years; older and larger specimens less often. Signs that a tree needs repotting include slow passage of water through the soil, or slowing of growth, or roots that appear like a coconut-fiber mat when the tree is eased from the pot. On the other hand, if you remove a tree from its pot after several years and see no roots at the edge of the soil mass, something is wrong. In such a case, all the old soil should be thoroughly washed from the roots and replaced with fresh, open soil at the earliest

Above: Begin to ease the tree from its pot by gently tilting it to one side. Never pull directly upward as this will surely damage the thicker roots

Right: When combing the roots, start at the edge and work your way to the center. Always comb outward, and take your time – rushing the job will damage heavy roots

48

each season is different and plants begin to stir in a different sequence from one year to another. However, generally speaking, deciduous species should be repotted first, and conifers up to a month later.

Repotting can be carried out during autumn – most traditional gardeners would recommend this time of year – but if you repot in autumn the pruned roots will have to endure the rigors of winter before they can begin to heal and regenerate. There is a considerable risk that the roots will die back and decay after autumn repotting, so such trees will need to be kept frost-free and watering kept to a minimum until spring.

Top and right: In ideal conditions a bonsai will produce masses of fine feeding roots. Using sharp scissors, cut these back until the remaining mass is about ¾ inch (20 mm) smaller all around than the inside of the pot

How to repot

1. First, gently ease the tree from its pot. If the pot has a lip on the inside of the rim you may need to use a sharp knife to cut around the edge of the root mass before removing it. If the root mass is stubborn, try pushing it out with a stick passed through the drainage holes. Avoid pulling the trunk too hard, as this can strain roots.

Using a metal hook, knitting needle or something similar, begin to "comb" away the roots and soil. Start at the edge and work all around, untangling the roots as you go. Always draw the hook outward, not across the surface of the soil, otherwise you may scar valuable surface roots. Take your time and avoid tearing at the roots.

2. Once you have untangled all the roots around the edge, you can begin to comb out the underside of the root mass, again working from the center outward. Give the tree a gentle shake every so often to remove loose soil. Continue untangling the roots until about a half of the soil has been removed from around the edge and the base of the trunk has been exposed underneath.

allow the remaining thinner roots to hang freely. These must now be trimmed with sharp scissors. If there are masses of fine roots they can be trimmed to a shape that fits comfortably in the pot, with a ½-¾ in. (10–20 mm) space all around the edges and underneath. If the fine roots are sparse, trim off about a third and fold the remainder underneath when replacing the tree in the pot.

6. Clean the pot with detergent, rinse it thoroughly and cover the drainage holes with mesh.

This latter point is extremely important, otherwise the tree will gradually "rise" in the pot at each successive repotting.

3. At this stage it is a good idea to spray the roots, first to keep them moist, second to wash away all soil residue so you can get a better view of the root structure, which will help when you begin to prune. I have now adopted the policy of washing away all old soil with a hose every second or third repotting. This not only ensures fresh, healthy soil right up to the trunk and removes any undesirable organ-

isms, but it also enables me to examine the whole root system for signs of decay and improve its structure by accurate selective pruning.

4. Now you can begin to prune the roots. Use a very sharp tool. If you have washed away all the loose soil the tool will retain its edge; if you haven't, the grit clinging to the roots will soon blunt it. Begin by pruning all the thick roots that have grown to the edge of the pot. Cut these back by between a third and a half, cutting back the thickest roots the furthest. You will remove a certain amount of fine feeding roots in the process, but new ones will grow from around the pruning cuts.

5. Hold the tree up and

Above: Thoroughly clean the pot before securing the drainage mesh with wire. Some pots have special holes for the retaining wires. If yours does not, pass the wires through the drainage holes

Right: Add a thin drainage layer of grit, then a layer of fresh soil, at least ½ inch (12mm) thick. Mound the soil slightly where the trunk will sit

Left: Settle the tree in position and secure it by pulling the retaining wires over the roots and twisting them together

Left: Work fresh soil between the roots with a pointed stick. Make sure that all voids have been filled, especially underneath the outer roots

Left: Level off the soil, leaving the surface just below the rim of the pot, and water well. After watering, the soil may settle further and you may need to add a little more to make up the level

Thread some wire through the drainage holes for use later to hold the tree firmly in the pot until the new roots have stabilized it. In large pots you can add a drainage layer of coarse grit or gravel, but in smaller pots this isn't necessary. If your soil is free-draining enough, a drainage layer shouldn't be necessary at all.

7. Place a layer of soil in the base of the pot, mounding it slightly where the trunk will sit – slightly off-center looks best. This layer should be deep enough to allow room for new roots to grow, but not so deep that the base of the trunk is raised above the rim of the pot, which would make efficient watering very difficult. You may need several attempts before you get it right.

8. Place the tree in the pot with the base of the trunk on the mound of soil, and settle it in by rotating the trunk back and forth a few times while applying gentle downward pressure. Once you are satisfied with the position of the tree in the pot, draw the wires over the roots and twist them together – not too tight – until the tree is held firm. These wires can be cut off in a couple of months, so leave the twisted ends where you can get at them when the time comes.

9. Add more soil, working it between the roots with a sliver of wood or a pencil (or a chopstick, if you wish to be authentic). Be gentle and don't stab at the soil. Guide the stick between the roots and move it in a circular direction so that soil is worked into all the spaces between, *and under* the roots as well as around the edges. Tap the sides of the pot with your fist from time to time to settle the soil further.

10. Finally, bring the surface of the soil to a level just below the rim of the pot and water well. A good soaking is crucial at this stage to ensure that all the new soil is thoroughly wetted. Place the tree in a sheltered position, away from direct sun, cold drafts, and frost, until the buds have begun to open. Don't feed for at least a month after repotting; allow the roots to recover their strength first.

Selecting a pot

Normally you would replant your bonsai in the same pot each time you prune the roots, but occasionally you may want to choose another one. Perhaps the tree has outgrown its original pot, or perhaps the color or shape no longer suit the tree. The variety of shapes, sizes, and colors is enormous, making the decision difficult. To a certain extent, the choice of pot depends on your personal taste, but there are a number of points to bear in mind which will make the decision easier.

Above: These rare antique Chinese bonsai pots are a far cry from the more subdued designs and glazes that are popular today. However, their beauty makes them collector's items in their own right

Opposite: Nests of more modestly-priced modern bonsai pots

Size and shape

A good bonsai pot will have generous drainage holes, a level base (to prevent pooling of water) and small feet to allow excess water to run away freely. It should not be glazed on the inside.

• In principle, slender trunks and group plantings look best in shallow pots, whereas thick trunks need deeper pots to maintain visual balance.

• Graceful, lowland styles of tree are set off best in oval pots or "soft-cornered" rectangles with a curved profile. Strong, angular, or gnarled trunks need equally strong rectangular-shaped pots.

• Wide, spreading styles look good in pots that flair outward at the top or have a lip on the outer rim. Tall, slender trees are complimented by very simple, round pots.

• For the pot to be in correct visual proportion, it should be slightly narrower than the spread of the tree.

• Bonsai that cascade over the side of the container should be planted in special deep pots. Cascade pots are not only more suited to that style, but they are infinitely more practical. They are also more horticulturally sound in that they allow the root structure to echo that of the branches.

Color

Bonsai pots are designed to compliment the bonsai. Highly glazed, brightly colored, or heavily patterned pots will distract attention from the tree itself and destroy the harmony of the composition.

• Species with delicate foliage such as Japanese maples or zelkova look good in pots with subdued

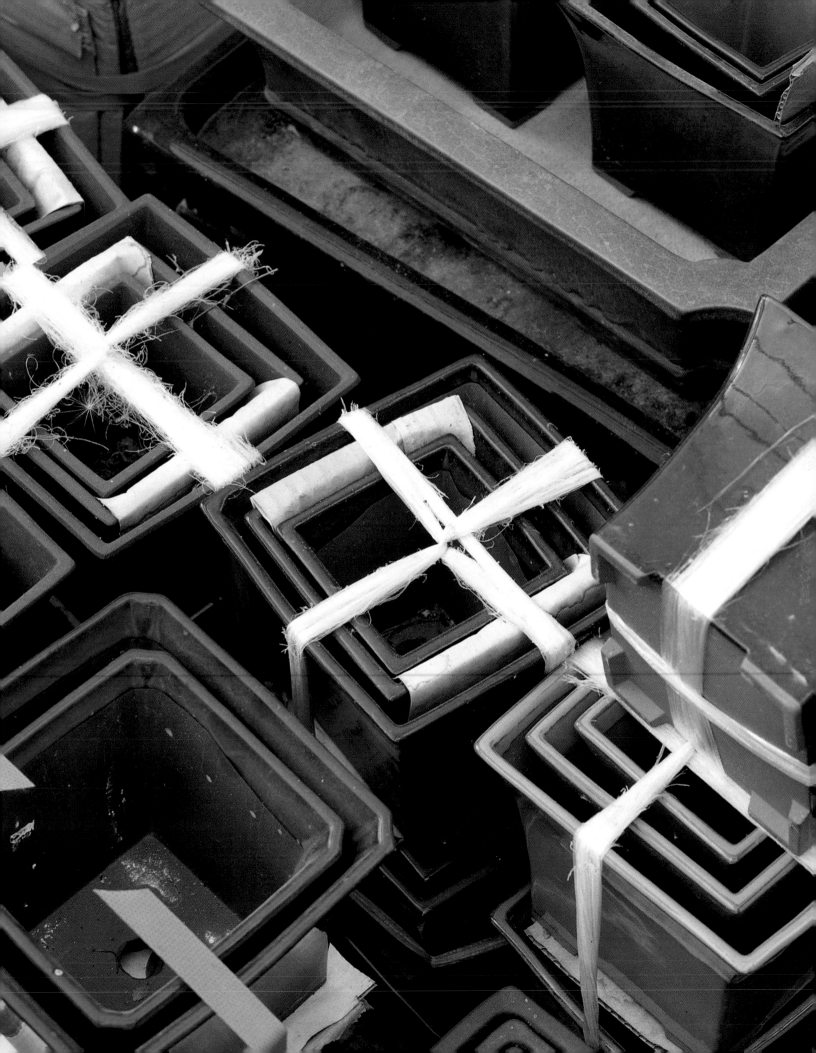

• To balance the extremely powerful effect of a flowering bonsai in full bloom, a more highly colored pot is required. The choice of color depends on your personal taste, but avoid really bright colors and high-gloss glazes. Consider the color of the flowers and try to compliment it. The exception to this rule is azaleas, which are treated as non-flowering bonsai as far as the choice of pot is concerned.

pastel glazes. Elms, serissas, azaleas, and dark-leaved deciduous trees can take a deeper color.

• Junipers and yews, with their chestnut-red bark, look good in subtle beige, brown, or burnt-umber colors with a matte, unglazed finish.

• The rich green needles and dark, craggy bark of pines are complimented by rich browns or deep reds with natural surface textures.

Opposite top: Bonsai pots are made in a bewildering variety of shapes, sizes, and colors

Opposite bottom: Oval glazed pots suit zelkovas, maples, and other graceful deciduous species

Above left: Tall pots are specifically designed for cascade or semi-cascade styles

Above right: Round "drum" pots are visually strong and suit tall, rugged pines

Left: These rectangular pots with geometric details compliment strong, heavy-trunked conifers or evergreen broad-leaved species

Choosing the right fertilizer

All green plants require the three main plant nutrients – nitrogen, phosphorus, and potassium – in order to thrive. An inadequate diet will cause symptoms such as general loss of vigor, poor flowering, and reduced resistance to disease. A total absence of any one of these three will eventually cause the plant to die. They also need minute quantities of a number of trace elements such as magnesium, zinc, boron, molybdenum, and so on. Although only needed in minute amounts, a deficiency of magnesium, for example, retards chlorophyll production, thus weakening the plant. Ensuring that your trees get a balanced diet has been made easy by the wide, if sometimes bewildering, range of commercial products currently available to the gardener.

What type of fertilizer?
Fertilizers can be divided into two main types: organic and inorganic. Organic fertilizers are manufactured from plant or animal remains. Bone meal, dried blood, farm-yard manure, and garden compost all fall within this cat-

egory. Inorganic fertilizers are manufactured from synthetic ingredients. As far as the three major nutrients are concerned, either type is capable of providing all that is necessary.

Both organic and inorganic fertilizers can be divided again into two groups: those intended for garden use and those intended for house plants. Some house-plant fertilizers are intended to induce rapid, lush growth which is undesirable on a bonsai. Avoid any that make this specific claim. Granular or dry garden fertilizers are intended for use on open ground, not in small containers, so judging the correct amount is impossible. Only trial and error will tell you, and the errors could prove expensive!

On the other hand, liquid garden fertilizers can be sprayed onto the foliage, which is a surprisingly efficient way of feeding plants, and doses can be judged precisely. The major drawbacks of foliar feeding are that it is impossible in wet weather, and in dry weather foliar feeds tend to leave powdery deposits on the leaves.

The secret of success is to read the package carefully before committing yourself, and to ensure that the contents include nutrients in the desired proportion (see below) and at least six trace elements. If there are no trace elements you will have to apply a proprietary trace element supplement as well. Also check that the product is suitable for container-grown plants – either giving instructions for use as a foliar feed or stating application rates for a given volume of pot.

Bonsai fertilizers

These are basically no different from any other fertilizer, except that they are generally not as rich. They are formulated for all-around health and are ideal for general use.

The three major nutrients

On every package of fertilizer you should find reference to the NPK analysis. This tells you the strength and balance of the three major nutrients: nitrogen, phosphates, and potash.

N – nitrogen
Nitrogen is responsible for promoting strong stems and healthy, dark leaves. Lack of nitrogen will result in thin, weak shoots and small, yellow leaves which rapidly fall. Too much nitrogen produces sappy stems and large leaves, both of which are vulnerable to fungal attack. Nitrogen is used up rapidly and so must be regularly replenished.

P – phosphates
Phosphates are necessary for strong, healthy roots and for prolific fruit production. A deficiency reduces root growth causing general poor vigor and discolored foliage. Flowering bonsai which seem reluctant to set fruit should be given a fertilizer high in phosphates.

K – Potash
Potash balances the effects of nitrogen. It is essential to flower production as well as to promoting resistance to fungal disease and generally hardening the plant against harsh environmental and climatic conditions. Scorched leaf margins – common on hornbeams and maples – may sometimes be avoided by increasing the potash content of the fertilizer. Increase the potash for flowering plants that are slow to bloom.

Following the letters "NPK" will be three numbers such as: "NPK 7:8:8." These give the proportion of each ingredient and the strength of the fertilizer. For instance, NPK 7:8:8 contains seven parts of nitrogen, eight of phosphates and eight of potash. It is a well-balanced food and is not too strong for bonsai. A product with NPK 25:15:15 is not only too high in nitrogen but is also too rich for our purposes. Fertilizers with high NPK values should be diluted to half-strength or even weaker.

What to use when

The first point to remember is not to feed your trees more than they can use or when they don't need it, such as in autumn. Either could easily "burn" the roots. This happens when the concentration of nutrients in the soil water is stronger than that within the roots. By the process of osmosis, water will pass from the roots back into the soil to balance the two solutions, killing the roots and causing the plant to suffer symptoms of drought (see page 30).

Secondly, the recommended rates of application for general fertilizers is calculated for vigorous growth on plants growing in normal potting composts. Bonsai soils are very free-draining and contain a large proportion of grit which cannot absorb nutrients for later use, and we want controlled rather than vigorous growth. It is usually better to use general fertilizers at half-strength, but applied twice as often as recommended. The proportion of each of the three nutrients and the timing of application will depend on the species and the desired results. The charts show the three basic feeding programs. However, there are some additional considerations to bear in mind.

Most evergreens are slightly active during winter and will benefit from an application of low-strength, slow-release fertilizer such as bone meal or organic fertilizer pellets applied in late autumn. Foliar feeds take effect too rapidly for this time of year.
• Broadleaved species which are in the development

stage will grow more vigorously with added nitrogen. Be sure to harden off the shoots with nitrogen-free feeds in late summer and autumn.

• High-nitrogen foods applied in late summer will cause soft growth which will be killed off by the first hard frost, or will wilt over winter on indoor bonsai. High-nitrogen foods also retard flower bud production.

• Increasing the phosphate content can aid recovery of weak or recently repotted trees. It will also encourage prolific fruiting on species such as *cotoneaster, malus, pyracantha,* and so on.

• Nitrogen-free fertilizer, applied in late summer and early autumn, checks late growth, thickens trunks and branches, and hardens the plant in readiness for winter.

• Feeding pines with nitrogen-free fertilizer in spring and high-nitrogen in late summer will encourage small needles and prolific back-budding.

• Flowering species that are reluctant to bloom should be given extra potash throughout the growing season until the problem is rectified. Increasing the potash in the tree's diet also encourages thickening of trunks and branches.

More detailed advice of feeding particular species is included in the Tree Directory.

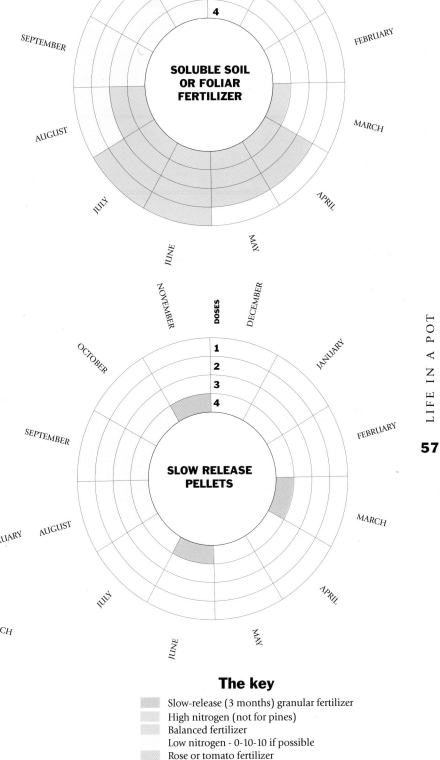

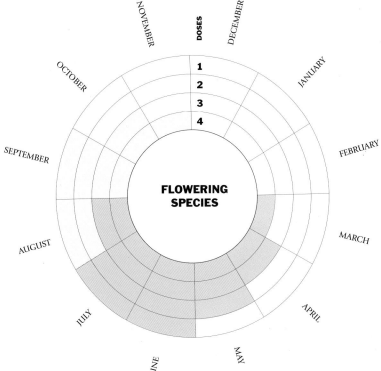

The key

	Slow-release (3 months) granular fertilizer
	High nitrogen (not for pines)
	Balanced fertilizer
	Low nitrogen - 0-10-10 if possible
	Rose or tomato fertilizer
	Slow-release for pines only

Keeping in trim

All commercial bonsai are, to a certain extent, mass-produced, so regardless of how much you pay, your bonsai will certainly have a number of imperfections which need to be rectified. There may be too many branches, or perhaps some will need repositioning. The younger twigs will almost certainly need attention – either now or in the near future. Remember, too, that bonsai are living plants that grow each year and this new growth must be controlled in order to maintain the perfect shape.

Pruning branches

Pruning branches on bonsai is a straightforward operation that requires just a little more care than pruning an ordinary garden shrub. With normal garden pruning, the wound heals rapidly as the trunk thickens, but on a bonsai the process is slower. What's more, the healing tissues can form an unsightly swelling that would soon disappear on a full-sized tree, but will remain indefinitely on a bonsai. To avoid this, follow these simple steps.

Always prune in spring, when the tree is active and healing can begin at once. Autumn pruning may result in die-back of surrounding bark, and summer pruning will cause unwanted shoots to grow from around the wound. First cut the branch as close as you can to the trunk without damaging the bark on the trunk itself. Use sharp, "bypass" clippers if you don't have special bonsai tools.

Using a wood-carver's gouge or strong modeling knife with a curved blade, begin to hollow out the wound. Work from the outside of the wound toward the center – and keep your fingers out of the way in case the gouge slips! Inspect the wound from all angles periodically until you are satisfied that, from the side, the edge of the wound is flush with the trunk.

Continue hollowing until the cavity is about two or three annual rings deep. This ensures that, as the new, swollen healing tissue covers the wound, it "rolls" into the cavity. By the time it has met in the center of the wound it will be flush with the surrounding bark.

The fresh wound must be sealed as soon as possible. Japanese cut-paste is perfect for the job, but a home-made substitute will do just as well. Mix some red and green modeling clay until it more or less matches the color of the bark, then add a little vegetable oil to prevent it from hardening. Press this evenly all over the wound, making certain that all the edges are well-covered. As the wound heals, the plug of paste will be pushed off. Never use bitumen-based sealants or any other type that dries hard. These always stain the bark and can cause further damage when you try to remove them.

Regeneration Pruning

If you have a branch that is too long, or has no side branches, or only bears foliage at the very end, you can rectify this by shortening the branch in mid-summer. At this time of year the tree's growth is in full flood and new shoots will spring from around the wound and, perhaps, further back along the remaining part of the branch. On branches that are less than ¼ in. (5-6 mm) thick it is advisable to prune to an internode, or set of leaf scars, which on the majority of species remain visible for several years. Conveniently, by the time the internodes disappear, the branch is mature enough to be pruned at any point with confidence. Seal the wound with cut-paste as described above.

This technique is only suitable for deciduous species. On conifers, the offending branch should either be removed completely and a replacement wired into position from elsewhere, or you could try to introduce more curves in the branch to bring the side branches and foliage closer to the trunk.

Pinching out new growth

In order to maintain neat, clearly defined foliage pads, it is essential that the tree readily produces new buds on old wood so that the resulting shoots can be used to replace areas of foliage that have become overcrowded or have outgrown the design of the tree.

Deciduous trees
The new shoots that emerge in spring first bear two or three small leaves. As the shoot extends, each new leaf increases in size. To maintain small leaves and to keep the tree in shape you must stop these new shoots from extending before the leaves become too large.

Left: Prune branches close to the trunk and carve away the stub, leaving a slightly hollow wound. Seal all wounds immediately

You may need some tweezers for this job – unless you have nimble fingers. All you need to do is to wait until the shoot has two or three true leaves, and then simply pinch out the tiny, soft tip. The shoot will grow no longer and the leaves will remain small. After a few weeks another flush of smaller shoots will grow from latent buds as well as the buds in the axils of the remaining leaves.

If you allow the shoots to grow too long before pinching, you will then have to use scissors and cut back to two or three leaves. But beware, cutting back an older shoot can cause the next flush of growth to be too "leggy" with large leaves.

If you want to extend a branch, let the shoot grow to the desired length and cut it back by half. Repeat this process with the next flush of shoots, and so on, until you resort to tip-pinching once again.

Junipers

Junipers either have scale-like foliage pressed tightly to the shoots, or sharp needles, generally borne in threes at each internode. To confuse the matter, junipers with scale-like foliage resort to needles following stress. This is known as juvenile foliage. All shoots bearing juvenile foliage should be pinched back in their first season, or cut out completely if there are only a few of them. If pinched in their second year, these shoots will wither and die without producing any new growth.

Pinching the normal shoots is done in one of two ways, depending on the nature of the shoot.

Extension shoots are much plumper and generally paler in color than the surrounding shoots. These should be cut back hard, right into last year's growth or even further. Cut back to a healthy pair of side shoots.

To keep the foliage clouds neat, the tip of all other shoots must be broken off. (Using scissors for this job will make the cut tips turn brown.) Grasp a fan of foliage between the thumb and finger of one hand and pull away the tips with the other. Rolling the tips as you pull helps them to break cleanly. This process is quite time-consuming and should be repeated several times during the growing season, which can continue long after deciduous trees have adopted their autumn color.

Flowering bonsai

If you pinch out the tips of flowering bonsai in the same way as other deciduous species, you will prevent the formation of next year's flower buds. With the exception of azaleas and some tropicals, the flower buds are formed at the base of the previous season's shoots.

To maximize next year's blossoms, trim to shape immediately after flowering and allow all new growth to grow unchecked until mid to late summer. Once the shoots have stopped extending, examine the buds at the base carefully. You should be able to see that they are rounder or larger than those further along the shoot.

Right: Once deciduous shoots have grown two full leaves, pinch out the soft growing tip

Center and below: To extend a branch, allow one shoot to grow until it begins to harden, then cut it back to the point where you want the first fork to be

These are the flower buds. Cut the shoots back, leaving two or three of these buds.

Next year, the new shoots that are produced from the base of the flowers will be short – perhaps only bearing two or three leaves. These are the beginnings of flowering spurs that do not extend but continue to bear flowers year after year, until they eventually become so crowded that they need to be thinned out.

Azaleas

Azaleas are valued not only for their flowers, but also for their neat foliage and strong trunks and branches. Commercial azaleas are invariably varieties of Japanese Satsuki azalea, whose flower buds are produced at the tips of last year's shoots and open after this year's have already begun to grow.

Immediately after flowering, cut back into last year's growth, removing the spent flower head and any new growth that emerged at its base. Ideally you should allow a few of last year's leaves to remain. It is a good idea, at this stage, to thin out last year's shoots, leaving only two at each fork. This prevents overcrowding and encourages new buds to form on

old wood, from which replacement branches can be built in the future.

Any over-vigorous extension shoots should be cut back to the base.

Pines

Pines have a unique growth pattern. In the wild, most pines rarely throw out new growth from old branches, and only do so in response to damage or stress. Here lies the answer. Bonsai growers developed a pruning technique which, by utilizing and controlling the tree's response mechanism, enables them to encourage pines to produce buds where they are needed with a fair degree of predictability. The secret is in the timing.

First stage: in spring, pine buds don't actually open to allow the embryonic shoot to emerge. Instead, they gradually elongate, tearing the fragile, papery sheath that protects them. (These elongating shoots are called "candles" for fairly obvious reasons.) As the sheath disintegrates, you will see tiny bright green "scales," which are the developing needles. We will call this the first stage.

Second stage: By the time the candles reach about half of their eventual length the groups of needles, about 1/8-1/4 in. (2-6 mm) long, start to slowly peel away. When they stand at about a 20-degree angle to the candle, they begin to separate into individual needles, still bright, fresh green. This is the second stage.

Right: On junipers, a few shoots will appear fatter and grow more rapidly than others. These should be cut back hard, leaving just one or two side shoots

Middle: To pinch the remaining foliage, grasp tufts of shoots between finger and thumb, and pull off the tips

Bottom: After stress, junipers produce uncharacteristic juvenile foliage. Isolated juvenile shoots can be cut out. Larger areas should be lightly pinched, and the shoots removed only when sufficient adult foliage has developed to replace them

Opposite: Spring flowering deciduous species such as crab apples and cherries must be allowed to grow unchecked until late summer, when they are cut back to leave only the flower buds at the base

Third stage: the candles elongate further and the needles lengthen and separate entirely from each other, darkening in color as they do so. The semi-mature needles are almost as dark as last year's, but only half the length of full-grown needles, and are still shiny and slender. This is the third stage.

Fourth stage: finally, if left untouched, by midsummer the shoots are fully mature. The needles have darkened and lost some of their sheen, and now stand well away from the shoot. The shoot itself has lost its juvenile green color and has turned a pale brown or gray color – the fourth stage.

Cause and effect

By timing the pinching-out of all or part of the candles, you can achieve different results, but there are a few points to remember before you begin.

Always start with the lowest, therefore the weakest, branch, and do the smallest candles first. This process guarantees that they will get a fair share of the healing auxins before the more vigorous candles are pruned.

• Do all the small candles on the tree first, spreading the work over a week or so. Then return to the stronger candles on the lowest branch and so on.

• Vary the amount you break off according to the comparative size of the candle. Break about one-third off the small candles and at least two-thirds off the very largest. You can increase this if you wait until stage three before beginning pruning.

• Where there are clusters of shoots in close proximity, remove some entirely, leaving no more than two shoots emerging from the same point.

If you begin candle pruning as the first stage of growth reaches completion, two or three buds will form at the wound during the summer, and perhaps at the base of the shoot. They will be large and vigorous and will grow strongly next year.

By the time you have finished, the larger candles will be almost at the end of stage two. Pruning shoots at this time will help promote new buds on last year's growth – ideal for replacing the over-vigorous shoot you have just pruned.

Pruning towards the end of stage three will reduce the vigor of the shoot and will result in a larger number of much smaller buds at its base and on last year's growth, possibly on two-year-old wood as well. There will be extremely few, if any, buds produced at the wound.

By late summer the shoot is fully mature and next year's buds have begun to develop. At this time you can remove the

shoot completely, leaving only a short stub (provided there are sufficient old needles remaining to nourish the branch). In healthy trees this will result in a mass of tiny buds forming during the winter on wood several years old. These buds are extremely delicate and difficult to spot, and will need two seasons' growth before they are strong enough to be trained as replacement branches.

Needle pulling

Old needles should be removed periodically by pulling them out one-by-one. This allows light and air into the tree and makes new bud production more prolific. It also

Above: As pine buds extend in late spring, they must be pinched back by bending them until they snap cleanly

Right: A strict regime of pinching and needle pulling will encourage the formation of adventitious buds on older parts of the branches. These are essential to build up density of foliage and to replace overgrown areas in the future

allows you to assess the branch structure and to apply wire if necessary. Remove more needles from the top of the tree than from the lower branches, thereby countering the tree's natural tendency to concentrate its energy in the apex. Autumn or early spring are the best times for this.

Shaping with Wire

The principle behind wire-training bonsai is simple. If a piece of wire of an appropriate thickness is coiled around a branch, the two together can be bent and the wire will hold the branch in position. As the branch grows, it thickens as new wood is produced. This new wood conforms to the new shape of the branch. In addition, the pressure of the wire on the bark increases as the branch thickens, and the wood beneath it becomes compressed and much more dense. The combination of these two factors means that after a suitable period, the wire can be removed and the branch will remain in place.

The length of time it takes for a branch to set depends on the species, the season, and the thickness of the branch. More detailed information is given in the Plant Index, but as a general principle, young deciduous shoots and twigs can set within a matter of a month or so, but springy conifer branches can take several years.

Once positioned, check the branches regularly, especially at the top of the tree where the growth is strongest. As soon as the wire appears to be biting into the bark, remove it immediately before it causes ugly scars. If the branch has not set satisfactorily, re-wire it, coiling the wire in the opposite direction to minimize the damage to the bark.

Always cut the wire off with sharp wire cutters that are able to cut right to the tip of the jaws. It may seem easier and certainly more economic to uncoil the wire, but this often tears the bark, and is certainly a false economy in the long run.

What wire?

In Japan, annealed (softened) copper wire is invariably used for all conifers, because of its greater holding power, and aluminum wire for deciduous trees. In the West, aluminum wire is used for all species by most enthusiasts simply because it is much cheaper, even when used double on heavier branches. Special brown, anodized aluminum wire is stocked in many sizes by all bonsai suppliers.

However, if you have access to offcuts of electrical cable, you can salvage copper wire in a variety of sizes. This can be annealed by heating it in a bonfire until it is red-hot and then quickly submerging it in cold water for a couple of seconds. The action of coiling it around the

1. The wire should be coiled at a 45 degree angle, in contact with the bark but not so tightly as to bruise it

2. On long branches or trunks, the wire used for the base may be too thick to use further along. You can transfer to thinner wire at a convenient point, overlapping the two by several turns to ensure good anchorage

3. When wiring a single branch, anchor the wire firmly by coiling it around the trunk several times

4. Better still, use one piece of wire for two nearby branches. Make sure both ends of the wire go through each "fork" in the same direction, as shown

5

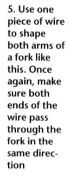

5. Use one piece of wire to shape both arms of a fork like this. Once again, make sure both ends of the wire pass through the fork in the same direction

6

6. Here two parallel wires have been used to shape the thick part of the branch. Then one is diverted to shape a side branch while the other continues along the main branch

7. When bending wired branches, use your thumbs as a fulcrum. Try not to make too sharp a bend at first

7

8. Once the branch has set, or when the wire has become too tight, it should be cut off. Never try to unwind the wire as you will risk damaging the bark

8

9. Leaving the wire on the branch for too long will cause scars which will take many years to heal – if ever. It may even become completely buried. These scars were made eight years ago and still have a long way to go

9

branch, then bending the branch and wire together, work-hardens the wire, more than doubling its strength.

Plastic-coated iron wire, sold in garden nurseries for tying up climbers and so on, is too rigid for bonsai use. Also, as it is coiled around the branch, the plastic coating tends to rupture, causing the core to rust, which then stains or even corrodes the bark.

How to wire

Before you begin, practice on a twig cut from a garden shrub until you have gained a little confidence. Then test the branch you are about to wire for its resistance, and try to find the thickness of wire that is slightly stiffer. You will find that it takes only a short while to become quite expert at gauging the right thickness of wire for any given branch.

Cut a piece of wire that is at least one-and-a-half times as long as the branch.

Deadwood on bonsai

In nature, many old conifers, especially those living in mountainous regions, display areas of deadwood which have become bleached by the sun and contrast dramatically with the colors of the bark and foliage. Caused by storms, drought or natural die-back, the deadwood tells us about the harsh conditions the tree has had to endure.

Japanese masterpiece junipers and pines, which have been developed from plants collected from the mountains, invariably have large areas of deadwood and are consequently highly prized. The deadwood is further refined or extended by the artist using a variety of carving techniques until, in some cases, an almost abstract design is achieved.

Commercial conifer bonsai, particularly junipers, have artificially created deadwood areas, either whole branches (in bonsai terms these are called *jins*) or on parts of the trunk (*sharis*). These relieve the visual monotony and also greatly enhance the bonsai's dynamic image.

Jins and sharis

Creating your own jins and sharis is quite a simple process, but should only be done after careful consideration. Too much deadwood, clumsily handled, will detract from the overall appearance of the bonsai and will be impossible to rectify. Jins and sharis can be made at almost any time of year, provided that the tree can be kept in frost-free conditions until the wounds have healed. But the best time is in late summer, when the sap is not rising so quickly and the wounds are less likely to "bleed." Also, at this time of year, the wounds still have time to heal before winter and the exposed heartwood will dry out within a few weeks.

If the wire is to hold the branch securely it must first be firmly anchored. Do this by coiling it a couple of turns around the trunk – or around the parent branch, if wiring secondary growth. Begin coiling the wire around the branch at an angle of about 45 degrees. Hold each turn of the wire with one hand while you coil the next to avoid exerting too much pressure on the bark.

Bend the branch by using your thumbs as fulcrums on the inside of the curve and spreading the pressure of your fingers along as much of the branch as possible. Bend in stages, listening carefully for cracking bark, at which point stop! If the branch has still not achieved the desired position, return to it every two or three weeks and bend it a little further until you are satisfied.

Above: The intricate grain of exposed heartwood, bleached and preserved, can add character and a sense of mystery to an otherwise mundane tree

**MAKING
A JIN**

Top: To
make a jin,
first cut
through the
bark around
the base of
the branch
stub, then
cut along its
length. The
bark should
peel away
quite easily

Middle:
Next, crush
the end of
the stub
with pliers
and peel
away strips
of wood to
expose the
inner grain

Below:
When fin-
ished, the jin
should
appear nat-
ural, as if the
branch had
broken in a
storm many
years ago

Jins

Once you have decided
which branch to covert to
a jin, shorten it to about
¾ in. (20 mm) longer than
the eventual desired length
of the jin. Then, with a
sharp modeling knife, cut
through the bark around
the base of the branch. Cut
right through to the heartwood making a vertical
"eye" shape. This will look
more natural when it has
healed and is less likely to
interrupt the flow of sap
past the jin.

• If you do this in spring or
summer, the bark on the
branch will come away
remarkably easily. Squeeze
the branch gently with pliers to separate it from the
heartwood and just pull it
off. If you try to create jins
in autumn or winter you
will have to scrape the
bark away with a knife
because, by this time, it
will have become fused to
the heartwood.

• The easiest way to create
a natural effect is to peel
away the surface layers of
heartwood to expose the
inner grain. Do this by
crushing the end of the jin
with the pliers and care-
fully pulling back small
sections of wood until the
desired effect is achieved.
As you near the base of the
jin be careful not to pull
too hard. Otherwise you
may find that you have
pulled away part of the
wood beneath the bark on
the trunk as well.

• Jagged splinters and
fluffy grain can be
removed by burning them
off with a candle flame or
something similar. The
heat from the flame will
also soften the resin in the
jin, enabling you to bend

it to a new position which
it will retain once the resin
has cooled. This heat-
bending technique can be
effective on jins up to two
or three years old!

Finally, the jin must be
preserved and bleached to
imitate the effect found in
nature. This is done with
the periodic application of
lime-sulphur compound
which penetrates the wood
and acts as a fungicide. The
foul-smelling liquid is yellow when applied, but as it
dries it turns silvery white.
Some brands dry too
white, and should be
mixed with a small
amount of black ink to
tone down the color.

Sharis

Sharis are best created in
mid to late summer when
the bark will peel away
easily. Before you start to
create a shari you must
first consider two very
important points: will the
removal of bark from the
chosen part of the trunk
retard the growth of any
branches growing immedi-
ately above it, and will the
shari appear natural?

To ensure that the shari
will not interrupt sap flow
to upper branches, exam-
ine the bark closely. You
should see faint swellings
in the bark, running verti-
cally. These indicate the
main sap-flow lines from
root to branch and, pro-
vided these are left more
or less intact, there should
be no problem. Junipers
and pines both have the

ability to transfer sap sideways to a certain extent, so you can afford to be a little daring here.

For the shari to appear natural, it should follow roughly the same line as the trunk. For example, if the trunk spirals to the left, make the shari do likewise; exaggerating the curves a little will make the shari more dynamic. Making the shari spiral in the opposite direction will not only look incongruous but will also risk interrupting the sap flow.

If possible, incorporate some existing or new jins in the shari for added interest and realism. Always ensure that some living bark is clearly visible on all parts of the trunk – ideally no less than 30 per cent of the width of the trunk should consist of living bark.

First mark the edges of the proposed shari with a water-based ink. (If you change your mind it will easily wash off.) Consider the lines carefully before you begin to work and only do so when you are perfectly satisfied that you are doing the right thing.
• Cut through the bark with a sharp modeling knife, following the line you have drawn and taking care not to let the knife slip. It is important to cut right through the bark at the first attempt in order to do a clean job – hence the need to stress the use of a *sharp* knife. Make a second cut about 2 mm inside the first, angling the knife so that the two cuts meet at the heartwood.
• The thin sliver of bark between the two cuts will

pull away easily, enabling you to insert another blade under the main part of the bark to be removed. This should now come away in one piece.
• Seal the exposed edges of the cut bark with cut-paste to retain moisture, and treat the exposed wood with lime-sulphur solution. Wetting the wood first with a fine spray helps it to absorb the lime-sulphur.

Once the exposed heartwood has dried you can add interest by carving or routing to emphasize the grain. I find that scraping the wood with a very hard wire brush or even a piece of broken glass creates an extremely natural and pleasing texture.

Maintenance

Jins and sharis require very little routine maintenance apart from an annual clean with a wire brush and the occasional application of lime-sulphur. However, as the years pass, the bark at the edges will encroach on the deadwood and would eventually engulf it completely if left alone. Every few years you will need to take your modeling knife and redefine the jins and sharis by cutting the bark back to its original position or beyond.

MAKING A SHARI

Top and center: For an more dramatic effect, you can strip the bark from one side of the trunk, incorporating several jins. Mark out the area first, making sure the shari follows the natural line of the trunk

Bottom: Once finished, sharis and jins should be treated with lime-sulphur to preserve and bleach the wood. Lime-sulphur smells strongly of rotten eggs so do this outside! The yellow solution fades to white as it dries

Tree Directory

Although all green plants require the same elements for survival – water, light, air, warmth, nutrients, etc. – they do not all require them in the same proportion. Furthermore, different species will react differently to training techniques such as pruning, wiring, and pinching. To ensure that you get the best from your bonsai it is important to know a little more about its unique idiosyncrasies.

Symbols

Hardiness

🌡 tender

🌡 half-hardy

🌡 tolerates light frost

🌡 tolerates heavy freezing

Difficulty

◩ easy

◩ need special care

◩ difficult

Sun/Shade

☀ full sun

◑ semi-shade

● shade

Acer buergerianum Trident Maple

Outdoor

Trident maples are often planted with their thick roots clinging tightly to a rock, creating really dramatic images

Trident maples are common parkland and street trees throughout the Far East and are popular for their rapid growth and brilliant autumn color. The bark on older trees becomes gray and cracked, but when confined to a container it remains pale gray with a pink flush which compliments the neat mid-green foliage.

In Japan, where almost all commercial trident maples are grown, the species' naturally rapid growth and thick, fleshy roots are exploited to produce a wide variety of styles. In recent years the fashion has been for thick, tapering trunks with strong buttresses where the roots flair at the base. These are produced in the thousands for export – a trunk 2 ¼ in. (60 mm) thick being achieved in five or six years.

Forest or group plantings are also common, comprising relatively young plants of varying heights and thickness. The main attraction of these is the interplay between the trunks and the feeling of perspective that can be achieved through careful arrangement of the individual plants.

Trident maples are the kings of the root-over-rock style of bonsai. The tree is planted over a jagged rock, representing part of a mountainside or cliff face, and its roots clasp the rock tightly until they finally plunge into the soil. As the roots thicken with age, a process that is hastened by the sun-warmed rocks, they become welded together where they touch and create the illusion of immense age and strength.

Where to keep trident maples

Trident maples should be kept outdoors at all times except for during periods of heavy frost, when they will need to be brought into a frost-free shed. They can be displayed indoors for a few days at a time while they are in leaf.

Trident maples enjoy full sun so long as the roots are not allowed to become too dry, in which case the margins of the leaves will burn. It is best to provide some afternoon shade. Protect from strong winds at all times.

Maintenance

Repotting: Every one to three years in early spring. Trident maples are the first deciduous trees to come into leaf, often during February in the UK, especially if kept frost-free all winter. Thick roots can be hard-pruned, almost up to the trunk if necessary. A new crop of fine roots will grow within a few weeks. Use Akadama or the standard soil mix.

Pruning: Best done in very early spring, two weeks before repotting. Pruning branches in midsummer will induce prolific adventitious growth.

Pinching: Pinch out the tips of all new shoots when two complete leaves have formed. Repeat as necessary through the year.

Watering: Trident maples dislike any hint of dryness in the soil. Drench the soil each morning in summer and check the soil again late afternoon. If it is slightly dry just below the surface, water again. Keep soil moist but not wet in winter.

Feeding: Balanced food from bud-burst until late summer, followed by low- or zero-nitrogen food.

Beware! When the thick roots on trident maples are allowed to freeze solid they can literally burst, like water pipes. Preventing the soil from becoming too wet in winter helps considerably, but protection from hard frost should be mandatory.

Acer palmatum Japanese Maple

Outdoor

Japanese maples are among the most beautiful trees on earth. Their slender, arching branches support an open canopy of delicate lobed leaves, whose subtle colors intensify to brilliant reds and oranges in autumn. They are naturally very graceful and elegant trees, and this aspect is echoed in bonsai. Heavy trunks and rigid, geometric branch formations look entirely out of place with this species.

These maples are notori-ously variable when grown from seed, which means that there are countless different strains available for bonsai. It is not uncommon to find that each tree in a consignment differs in some way from the others. The leaves – which usually have five or seven lobes, can vary in spring from bronze, through orange, to bright red; turning to various shades of green in summer, often with red margins.

The shoots – often colored red or orange – are fine, and grow prolifically from internodes on old wood or from around pruning wounds. These clusters of shoots must be thinned out, leaving a maximum of two at any

Japanese maples are graceful, elegant trees with delicate leaves. This specimen *Acer palmatum* is planted in a pot by British ceramic artist, Gordon Duffett

one point. Failure to do this will result in swollen, knotty structures which will look unnatural and will spoil the elegance of your bonsai.

Large-scale production of commercial Japanese maple bonsai unfortunately leads to a number of poor-quality examples in each shipment. Faults such as uneven roots or ugly pruning scars are, sadly, not uncommon, so consider each tree carefully before deciding which one to buy.

Where to keep Japanese maples

Japanese maples should be kept outdoors at all times except during periods of heavy frost, when they should be brought into a frost-free shed. They can be displayed indoors for a few days at a time while they are in leaf or for an hour or so in winter.

Japanese maples will tolerate full sun as long as the roots are not allowed to become too dry, and they are not exposed to strong winds; otherwise the leaves will scorch. In practice, semi-shade and wind protection are advisable.

Maintenance

Repotting: Every one to three years in spring, as the buds begin to elongate and adopt a sheen. Use Akadama or the standard soil mix. Add some sphagnum moss in hard-water areas.

Pruning: Best done during the spring, two weeks before repotting. Pruning branches in midsummer results in masses of new shoots from the internodes.

Pinching: Pinch out the tips of all new shoots when two or four complete leaves have formed. Repeat as necessary throughout the year.

Watering: Japanese maples require slightly acid soil conditions, so use rainwater instead of tapwater if possible. Keep soil moist at all times, avoiding both waterlogging and dryness. Spray foliage regularly.

Feeding: Balanced food from bud-burst until late summer, followed by low- or zero-nitrogen food. Apply soil acidifier twice a year in hard-water areas

Beware! Aphids colonize young shoots in spring and distort the new leaves. In winter, a cold wind can kill fine shoots; in summer leaves can become scorched by little more than a gentle breeze, so protection from wind at all times is essential.

Acer palmatum "Kiyohime" Kiyohime Maple

Outdoor

"Kiyohime" maple bonsai are quite rare and consequently more expensive than other varieties of maple. Their rarity is due to their extremely slow rate of growth and their tendency to grow into a low, spreading shrub – both of which make bonsai culture difficult. The difficulty doesn't stop once the bonsai image has been achieved, either. Maintaining it requires a little more careful consideration and attention to detail than other maples. However, the trouble taken is worthwhile, because the tiny bright-green leaves and dense tracery of fine twigs can form a convincing image of a full-grown tree, even on very small bonsai.

"Kiyohime" are almost invariably grown as a "broom-style" bonsai, where all the branches emanate from more or less the same point at the top of a straight trunk and fan out in all directions, dividing and sub-dividing as they progress. "Kiyohime" look especially good in winter, when their fine twig structure is clearly visible.

Where to keep "Kiyohime" maples

Like all Japanese maples, this tree should be kept outdoors at all times. Although technically hardy, "Kiyohime" growing in containers are less tolerant of freezing and should be regarded as half-hardy, and so should be taken into a frost-free building when temperatures dip much below freezing. They can be displayed indoors for a few days at a time while they are in leaf or for an hour or so in winter.

"Kiyohime" maples are delicate and very easily scorched by sun or wind, so they must be protected from too much of either. Shadow, cast by a taller nearby structure such as a house or fence, is better than overhead shading. If overhead shade is too dense, the inherently weak apex on "Kiyohime" may lose vigor and die back.

Maintenance

Repotting: Every one to three years in spring, as the buds begin to elongate and show green between the scales. Keep absolutely frost-free after repotting.

Use Akadama or the standard soil mix. Add some sphagnum moss in hard-water areas to increase acidity.

Pruning: Prune in spring, two weeks before or after repotting. Thin out overcrowded branches and twigs. Never hard-prune the leader or the upward-growing branches that form the apex. "Kiyohime" have a natural horizontal

"Kiyohime" maples are naturally low, spreading shrubs and are ideally suited to this style of bonsai

habit and are notoriously reluctant to regenerate a wounded apex.

Pinching: Pinch out the tips of all new shoots when two or four complete leaves have formed. Repeat as necessary throughout the year. Allow the apex to grow a little more to gain vigor before cutting back to two leaves.

Watering: Japanese maples need slightly acid soil conditions, so use rainwater instead of tapwater if possible. Keep soil moist at all times, avoiding both waterlogging and dryness. Spray foliage regularly.

Feeding: Balanced food from bud-burst until late summer, followed by low- or zero-nitrogen food. Apply soil acidifier twice a year in hard-water areas.

Beware! Avoid all unnecessary damage to the branches that form the apex, as that part of the tree is weakest on "Kiyohime" and lacks the vigor to recover as well as other Japanese maples.

Acer palmatum "Deshojo/Chishio"
Japanese Red Maples

Not to be confused with the coarse and ugly "Atropurpureum" with dull purple foliage, these varieties are true red maples, whose leaves emerge bright scarlet in spring and return to that color again in autumn. Even the shoots are bright red and glow against the pale gray bark.

If kept in bright but not sunny conditions, the leaves can even remain red all summer, but in most years, either variety will display a variety of leaf colors at any one time –

older leaves becoming green, with red or orange margins or veins, and younger, fresher leaves flashing bright red. Cutting off all leaves in mid-summer will induce a frost crop of red leaves, smaller than the first. These leaves stand a better chance of remaining undamaged by autumn and are likely to produce a better autumn display. However, this should only be done on strong, healthy trees and even then only in alternate years.

Red maples are rather slow-growing – more so in containers – so, when buying, it is best to spend a little extra for a more developed tree.

True red maples are less vigorous than most other varieties and need extra protection from wind. The red spring color often fades toward green in summer but returns in autumn

Where to keep Japanese red maples

Keep red maples outdoors at all times except when temperatures dip much below freezing for more than a few days, when they should be taken into a frost-free shed. They can be displayed indoors for a few days at a time while they are in leaf or for an hour or so in winter. Even a few days indoors in spring can turn the bright red leaves to dull green, which they will remain until autumn.

Japanese red maples are fairly delicate and easily scorched by sun or wind, so they must be protected from too much of either. However, if kept in a sunny position the leaves might retain their gorgeous red color all summer. The trick is to provide shade from the afternoon sun by placing the bonsai in the shadow of a nearby tree or building. This ensures adequate light from overhead but manages to eliminate the hottest sun of the day.

Maintenance

Repotting: Every one to three years in spring, as the buds begin to elongate and shine. Keep absolutely frost-free after repotting. Use Akadama or the standard soil mix.

Pruning: Prune in spring, two weeks before or after repotting. Thin out overcrowded branches and twigs. Prune out old knots and spurs by cutting back to a conveniently situated shoot or bud which can be allowed to grow on as a replacement.

Pinching: Pinch out the tips of all new shoots when two or four complete leaves have formed. Repeat as necessary throughout the year. Allow late summer growth to grow unchecked to build up vigor before giving a final trim in early autumn, as the leaves begin to change color.

Watering: Japanese maples require slightly acid soil conditions, so use rainwater instead of tapwater if possible. Keep soil moist at all times, avoiding both waterlogging and dryness. Spray foliage regularly.

Feeding: Balanced food from bud-burst until late summer, followed by low- or zero-nitrogen food. Apply soil acidifier twice a year in hard-water areas.

Beware! Spray at monthly intervals against aphids, which are difficult to spot on red maples because they adopt the same color as the shoots. When protecting from wind, also ensure that there is adequate ventilation to all parts of the tree, as powdery mildew can be a problem when air circulation is poor, especially if the soil is kept too dry.

Arundinaria
Bamboo

Indoor

In recent years varieties of bamboo have become increasingly popular as subjects for indoor bonsai because of their typical oriental appearance, but they are seldom used by serious collectors either in China or Japan. Specimen bamboo bonsai are rare, and are always planted in large groupings on stone slabs or in large shallow trays, imitating the dense, swaying groves familiar in all Far Eastern countries.

Bamboos are grasses and, therefore, do not form branches and cannot be trained into tree-forms. Instead, new shoots emerge from below soil level to add to the grove and are pinched out at the

desired height. During the next few years the stems thicken and the tufts of foliage become more abundant, until eventually the stem becomes too bushy and has to be cut out at the base and replaced by a younger one.

If any one stem is allowed to become disproportionately large it will dominate the others. Bearing in mind that all the stems are growing from the same interconnected root system, dominant stems will take more than their fair share of water and nutrients until the smaller and weaker stems wither and die. This is the natural order of bamboo groves, but is not so desirable in bonsai.

Where to keep bamboo
Most varieties of bamboo are more or less hardy when grown in the ground, but in containers they are less tolerant of cold. Ideally all bamboo should spend their summers outside, but they are content to stay indoors

The supple stems of bamboo sway gracefully in the gentlest of breezes, evoking the true feeling of the Orient

year-round if they receive enough light and fresh air.

Keep your bamboo bonsai close to a sunny window, but positioned where it will be shaded from direct sun during the hottest part of the day. Outdoors, bamboo can receive as much sun as you like, provided the soil is not allowed to dry out.

Maintenance
Repotting: Every two to three years in spring or autumn. Cut "wedges" out of the dense, fleshy root system and either discard or replant them elsewhere. The remaining sections of root and stems can be rearranged in the pot to improve the design. Place the thickest stems toward the centre of the group and the smaller ones toward the rear and the sides, creating the illusion of perspective.

Use standard soil mix with a couple of extra handfuls of organic matter. If planting on a slab or rock, make sure that there are no hollows in the surface to trap water.

Pruning: Cut out overgrown or dominant stems just below soil level with a sharp knife. Unwanted new shoots can be plucked out when still young and soft.

Pinching: When each stem has achieved the desired height, (taller in the center of the group than at the edges), pluck out the growing tip with tweezers. Thin

out side growth to maintain a natural bamboo-like appearance.

Watering: Bamboo love moist soil but suffer from severe root rot in water-logged conditions. For this reason you must use a free-draining container and water frequently during hot weather – perhaps three or even four times a day in the height of summer. If this is not possible, use a deeper container which will require less frequent watering but will not be so aesthetically harmonious with the slender, graceful stems and foliage.

Feeding: Half-strength balanced fertilizer during the growing season with a low nitrogen top-up in autumn. A weak balanced food in winter will keep bamboo grown in warm homes in good condition.

Beware! Waterlogged soil will kill bamboo as quickly as drought.

Bougainvillaea
Bougainvillea

Indoor

Originally from South America, these semi-ever-green climbers are now a familiar sight in gardens throughout the Mediterranean region. Their colorful bracts, which are often mistaken for flowers, vary from white through all shades of pink to rich crimson and are borne in late summer to early autumn. The tiny flowers are nestled in the centers of these bracts.

As with all climbers, growth is straggly and collapses unless supported. To produce a large bonsai from this species, the plant has to be grown in open ground for many years until a thick trunk base develops, whereupon all growth is removed and the new branch structure can be grown and trained. This long-winded procedure makes worthwhile bougainvillea expensive, but nonetheless desirable.

Where to keep bougainvillea

Bougainvillea adore full sun throughout the summer months, whether indoors or out. Outdoors, however, it is less easy to control the water, and flowering may be inconsistent. (Without the flowers there would be no colorful bracts.) Bear in mind also that hot sun through window glass is intensified, so some light shade, such as an open-weave net curtain,

is beneficial in the hottest part of the day.

In winter keep bougainvillea on the cool side -- between 46.5 and 59°F (8 and 15°C), during which time some older leaves will be shed. If all the leaves fall, it is probably because the plant is in a draft, because it has been allowed to become too cold, or through over-watering. Move the plant to a more suitable position and watch the watering more carefully, and it will soon recover.

Maintenance

Repotting: Every three to five years in spring, removing as much of the old, spent soil as possible, but don't be too severe with pruning the roots. Climbers start life in the shade at the base of taller trees through which they will climb to reach the sun. Their fibrous roots are kept cool and moist by the rich, deep leaf litter in which they grow. Imitate these natural conditions by using a deeper than normal pot and increasing the organic content of the soil to 80 percent, keeping it coarse and well-aerated.

Pruning: Branch pruning can be carried out at any time while the plant is in its semi-dormant state. Prune current season's growth hard immediately after flowering. Spring growth should be allowed to grow unchecked until the first few leaves have hardened, when they are cut back to one or two leaves. The following flush of growth will bear the

flowers. Pruning too early will induce too much vegetative growth; too late will retard flowering. It may take a couple of years to determine the best time to prune, which will depend largely on its environment.

Watering: Allow the soil to become almost dry in winter. The surface can be allowed to become bone dry, but the color should darken slightly with moisture beneath. When buds begin to swell in spring, give a thorough watering and then keep the soil moist but never saturated. Bougainvilleas do not tolerate wet, airless soil.

Feeding: Low nitrogen food, such as rose or tomato fertilizer, monthly while the plant is growing. Stop feeding immediately

when the plant stops growing and resume when growth restarts in spring.

Beware! Moving your bougainvillea from one environment to another without gradual acclimatization can cause defoliation and retard flowering. Always introduce it to its new quarters in stages over a two-week period, increasing the time spent each day.

Below: Unlike many climbers, bougainvillea will readily produce a fine branch structure

Right: The colorful red bracts – often mistaken for petals – are the main point of interest of bougainvillea bonsai

Carmona can be difficult to maintain but makes an ideal species for indoors. This one is just about to flower

Carmona microphylla
Fukien Tea

Indoor

Some people find Fukien tea can be very hard to look after but can be an ideal species for indoor bonsai. This common Asiatic garden shrub will thrive in hot, steamy kitchens and sunny window sills that do not cool down at night, but it is quite easy to overwater.

The small, neat leaves are rich, glossy green and are borne on stout shoots that spring out from all parts of the tree. The shoots are so prolific that you can reshape the tree in a very short time simply by trimming it like a topiary hedge. Periodically the older foliage-bearing spurs must be thinned out to prevent inner growth from dying from lack of light and air. This provides an ideal opportunity to refine the branch structure and make a more tree-like framework to support the new foliage. Try to introduce spaces between different layers of foliage to make the tree look older and more dignified. Each time you do this your bonsai noticeably improves.

The small white flowers can appear at any time of year. Flowering is induced by heat and humidity – remember, this is a tropical plant of Chinese descent which is not attuned to our seasonal changes – so if you can maintain both at a sufficiently high level you will be rewarded by masses of flowers all year round. For best results, the temperature should not fall below 68°F (20 °C), even at night. Humidity should be kept high – stand the pot in a tray of water, supported on stones so that the drainage holes are clear of the water, to increase local humidity. This can be done all year round, indoors or out, and is an attractive way to display this bonsai.

Where to keep carmonas

Carmonas adore sunshine and perform poorly in even shady conditions. After acclimatization, your carmona can stay in full sun outside all summer, but should be brought in to a sunny window as soon as the nights become cooler. If kept indoors all summer, check that the afternoon sun through the glass is not burning the foliage, and reposition the tree if necessary. Avoid moving your carmona around too much as they dislike excessive fluctuations in temperature.

Maintenance

Repotting: Every two to three years in spring. Use a little extra coarse organic matter in the soil and water sparingly for a week or two after repotting to encourage the new roots to grow in search of moisture.

Pruning: Branches can be pruned at any time. Thin out congested areas to allow more light and air to penetrate and to induce fresh growth.

Pinching: Pinch out shoots that threaten to spoil the neat outline of the tree as the need arises.

Watering: Carmonas are moisture-lovers, so keep the soil well moistened in winter and water prolifically in summer. Spraying the foliage regularly will improve flowering. Plunge the pot in a bowl of water from time to time to avoid dry spots.

Feeding: Low nitrogen food whenever the tree is in active growth. In cool rooms growth may cease for a while in winter, in which case stop feeding until growth recommences.

Beware! Even the slightest hint of frost or icy draft can be fatal to carmonas. Treat for aphid infestations with insecticides especially recommended for indoor plants.

Carpinus Hornbeam

Outdoor

Varieties of hornbeam are found in most temperate regions of the world, but the two most commonly used for commercial bonsai production are *Carpinus laxiflora*, Japanese hornbeam, and *Carpinus turczaninowii*, Korean hornbeam – both produced mostly in Japan.

All hornbeams have neat, oval leaves with finely toothed margins and depressed veins, giving each leaf its own pattern of light and shade. The Japanese hornbeam has pale gray bark that develops wavy vertical streaks of paler gray, running from roots to apex, as the tree matures. This can often occur in relatively young bonsai and is one of this variety's most endearing features. The Korean hornbeam has a darker gray bark with hints of mahogany, but it remains featureless until very old. However, very few species can equal the vivid orange autumn color which more than compensates for the lackluster bark.

The fine twigs and elegant branches are deceptively supple – up to a point. They have an annoying habit of cracking when bent too far, without the usual increase in resistance of other species that warns you to be careful. So take extra care when wire-training, and bend each branch a little at first, then return at weekly intervals to bend it some more, until the final position is achieved.

Where to keep hornbeams

Hornbeams are theoretically tolerant of full sun, but in hot weather the roots do not seem to be able to draw water as quickly as it evaporates from the leaves. The result is scorching of the leaf margins; in severe cases the entire leaf may be destroyed. No amount of watering seems to prevent this from happening, so the solution is to position the tree where it will not receive any direct sun after late morning – if at all.

In winter you can leave your hornbeam outside in all weather with confidence, provided temperatures do not fall below 12.6°F (-7°C). In temperatures lower than this, take the tree into a shed or garage where the temperature is a few degrees higher. Don't allow the tree to stay for more than an hour or so in rooms above 41°F (5°C) or it might break dormancy too soon.

Above right and below: The gray-striped bark of Japanese hornbeam creates the illusion of an old tree, and is especially effective in forest plantings

Maintenance

Repotting: Every two years in spring, as buds begin to swell. Use Akadama or standard bonsai mix. (Provide extra shade and be extra vigilant with watering if using Akadama.)

Pruning: Branches can be pruned at any time between leaf-fall and spring. Thin out congested areas and shorten over-extended growth in mid-summer to induce rapid replacement growth.

Pinching: Pinch out tips of new shoots when two true leaves have formed.

Watering: Water copiously when in growth. Never allow the soil to become even slightly dry. In winter, maintain soil evenly moist.

Feeding: Balanced food from spring to late summer, followed by low-nitrogen or nitrogen-free food in autumn. Over-feeding can cause weak, sappy growth which is even more prone to scorch in the sun.

Beware! Hot sun and drying winds can have a devastating effect on the leaves of a hornbeam grown in a shallow container.

Celtis sinensis Chinese Hackberry

Outdoor

Chinese hackberries are deciduous trees with small oval leaves and fine twigs. The leaves and internodes (spaces between leaves on the shoot) reduce well in response to constant trimming and pinching, and back-budding is prolific, making this an ideal species for bonsai.

The flowers, which appear in spring, are small and insignificant, but the bright orange fruit is extremely attractive and unique among deciduous bonsai species. Having

said that, the fruit is reluctant to set in temperate climates so special treatment is needed to encourage better performance. Spray several times a day from spring onwards and place the tree over or close to a tray of water to maintain high local humidity. On cool evenings bring the tree into the kitchen so that both temperature and humidity are maintained. Even with this treatment, in poor summers the fruit may be sparse, but the good years certainly make up for the bad.

The strong yet graceful trunk of this *Celtis* provides a good base for the well-distributed branches and neat leaves

Where to keep a hackberry

Although fully hardy, the fact that most *celtis* bonsai originate in China and Taiwan means that they are generally imported by dealers in indoor bonsai and are often sold as such. They can survive well indoors all year round but must be kept below 46.4°F (8°C) during the winter to ensure that the tree has a sufficient dormant period. Placing it on a balcony or outside window sill which is sheltered from the wind is an easy solution. During summer your *celtis* will need to be close to an open sunny window if it is to remain healthy. Poor light and ventilation will result in weak, leggy growth and persistent attacks of powdery mildew.

Outdoors, the tree can receive as much sun as you like, provided the pot is shaded and the soil is not allowed to become even slightly dry.

In winter you can leave your hackberry outside in all weather with confidence, provided it is sheltered from the wind and temperatures do not fall below 9°F (-5°C). If they do, then bring the tree into a frost-free shed or garage.

Maintenance

Repotting: Every year in spring for younger trees, every 2 years for older specimens.

Use Akadama or standard bonsai mix with a little extra coarse organic matter or calcined clay to increase water retention.

(Provide extra shade and be extra vigilant with watering if using Akadama.)

Pruning: Branches can be pruned at any time between leaf-fall and spring. Thin out congested areas and shorten over-extended growth in mid-summer to induce rapid replacement growth, or in the dormant season for permanent removal of certain areas.

Pinching: Pinch out tips of new shoots when two true leaves have formed.

Watering: Water copiously when in growth. Never allow the soil to become even slightly dry. In winter, maintain soil evenly moist.

Feeding: Balanced food in spring followed by low-nitrogen for the rest of the growing season. Apply one nitrogen-free feed in autumn.

Beware! Chinese hackberry need permanently moist soil, but react badly to over-watering. Finding the right balance takes a little practice, but the inclusion of extra organic matter or water-retentive calcined clay to the soil will help.

Chaenomeles Flowering Quince

This garden shrub has long been one of the most popular winter-flowering plants in temperate regions throughout the world. During summer, it is a rather scruffy, multi-stemmed bush, with little appeal. But in late winter and early spring its apple-blossom-like flowers, ranging from pink to deep red with yellow centers, brighten the grayest of days long before the crocuses or daffodils appear. When planted against a sunny wall it will even flower before Christmas most years.

Quince's natural multi-stemmed habit is caused by its tendency to produce suckers – adventitious shoots that grow from the spreading roots. This habit persists even when quince is grown in a container, which makes training it as a normal single-trunked tree very difficult indeed, and the commercial examples that are produced will always be more trouble than they are worth.

Bonsai artists work with nature to produce a type of clump style which is unique to this species. After several years' growth in the ground, the developing plant is lifted and planted in a pot with the thick upper roots fully exposed. This also exposes the points of origin of the many suckers. Some are selected for training into trunks and the rest are pruned away. The trunks are trained by hard pruning to appropriate side growth every summer, which produces gnarled, angular trunks and short, stubby branches laden with flowering spurs.

Below: Regular hard pruning each year eventually produces gnarled, angular branches covered in masses of flower buds

Right: From Christmas through to late spring, the blossoms of flowering quince will reward you with a blaze of color

Where to keep flowering quince

Quince will thrive in full sun or in semi-shade, and will flower just as well in either. They are, however, not drought-tolerant, so shading the pot to prevent evaporation on hot days is a good idea.

My quince spends the entire winter outdoors every year and has survived temperatures of 30°F (-17°C) unscathed. Keeping it above 9°F (-5°C) at night and giving it plenty of sunshine during the day will encourage earlier flowering.

Maintenance

Repotting: Every one to two years in spring for younger trees, every three to four years for older specimens.

Use standard bonsai mix with a little extra coarse organic matter and a comparatively deep pot.

Pruning: Prune for branch structure immediately after flowering and allow all new shoots to grow unchecked until they stop extending – usually mid to late summer. At this point, cut them all hard back, leaving only the first two or three leaves. It is the buds in the axils of these leaves that will develop into new flowering spurs.

Pinching: Late season growth should be snipped back to one or two leaf nodes in autumn.

Watering: Water copiously when in growth. Never allow the soil to become even slightly dry. In winter, maintain evenly moist soil.

Feeding: Balanced food in spring followed by low-nitrogen for the rest of the growing season. Apply one nitrogen-free feed in autumn.

Beware! Chaenomeles are thirsty when grown in containers and are the first species to wilt if the soil begins to dry. This may not harm the tree permanently, but it can cause the new shoots to wither and die. Aphids love quince.

Chamaecyparis obtusa
Hinoki Cypress

In nature a hinoki cypress has a flame-shaped profile, but as the tree reaches maturity it adopts a broad, almost domed appearance with clouds of foliage supported above branches that have become bare and exposed. This is the image that most hinoki bonsai try to evoke, although the slow-growing nature of the species means that good examples are rare and expensive. Nevertheless, more reasonably priced trees can get you off to a good start, and are worth trying.

The scale-like leaves are edged with silvery-blue, and the shoots curl inward at the tips. The dense, compact shoots rapidly form billowing clouds of foliage which must be regularly and meticulously pinched throughout the growing season. Periodically they need to be thinned out – all dead leaves and shoots cleaned away and the central spine of all clusters of shoots cut back to two healthy side shoots. Failure to do this will eventually lead to long, meandering branches with tufts of green at the tips, and the bonsai will be ruined. Congested foliage is also perfect for red spider mites, which can devastate a tree in just a few weeks.

Where to keep hinoki cypress

Although tolerant of hot sun in the wild, in containers hinoki cypress are more happy in semi-shade during the hottest months. This probably has more to do with the temperature of the roots than the sun on the leaves.

Hinoki can withstand frozen roots for considerable periods provided the tree is not exposed to drying wind. The waxy coating provides some protection against wind, but not enough for containerized plants. It does, however, help the foliage to appear healthy long after the tree has died! Don't bring hinoki cypress into the house in winter – not even for an hour.

Maintenance

Repotting: Every two to three years in mid spring, depending on the age of the tree. Older specimens every five years. Use standard bonsai mix. Akadama can be used if you can guarantee never to let it dry out.

Pruning: Prune branches and thin old twigs in summer, when wounds will heal easily and foliage that has accidentally been knocked off will regrow quickly.

Most commercial *chamaecyparis* bonsai are created from dwarf varieties which readily produce sturdy trunks and masses of compact foliage

Pinching: Pinch out the growing tips of all shoots as soon as they begin to over-extend and spoil the neat outline of the tree. Grip a fan of foliage between thumb and forefinger and pull off the tips with the other hand. Repeat this as necessary, spraying regularly for a week or so after each session.

Watering: Hinoki cypress will not tolerate dry roots, and once they have been damaged by drought, they seldom recover, sometimes taking as much as three years of prolonged agony for you and your bonsai before eventually dying. So water well all year, being especially vigilant in sum-

mer and, of course, avoid waterlogging.

Feeding: Balanced food from spring until late summer, followed by nitrogen-free in early autumn. One dose of balanced, slow-release fertilizer in winter will help prepare the tree for spring. Apply all at half strength.

Beware! The fans of foliage on hinoki cypress are very easily dislodged when wiring or thinning out old twigs, so handle with care.

83

Cotoneaster horizontalis
Cotoneaster

Outdoor

Cotoneasters are almost too good for bonsai. Nearly everything the bonsai enthusiast wants is offered by this popular garden shrub. It has very small, glossy, dark-green leaves which turn shades of orange or red in autumn. In spring, the tiny, spherical flowers cover the tree with a mass of pink and white. Later in the year, bright orange or red berries are borne prolifically and can persist right through winter if the birds don't get them.

And there's more: in spring, or after pruning, a new straight shoot will grow from every single leaf axil which, over the years, creates a uniform herringbone pattern of twigs – rather like a fern frond in structure. This enables even the beginner to predict exactly where each new shoot will grow from and the direction it will take, making the develop-ment of good branch structures and neat, well-organized foliage clouds an almost boringly straightforward operation.

But there are two drawbacks. First, the growth of new shoots is so prolific that the regular trimming can become tedious. Second, the trunks and exposed roots are slow to thicken once the tree is growing in a container. If you are not satisfied with the thickness of the trunk on your cotoneaster, plant it in the ground for a couple of years and see the difference!

A similar variety, *cotoneaster microphyllus*, has evergreen leaves and white flowers that open completely like miniature apple blossoms.

Where to keep cotoneaster
Full sun all year round suits cotoneasters perfectly. Having said that, cotoneasters can be kept in semi-shade without any problems, but fruit may not set quite so well. They can also be displayed indoors for a few days at a time at any time of year without coming to apparent harm.

Cotoneaster are a perfect species for smaller bonsai. The minute leaves and colorful flowers and berries give year-round value

In winter you can leave cotoneasters outside in most kinds of weather provided they are sheltered from persistent rain and winds. If the temperature dips below 12.6°F (-7°C) for more than a day or so, take it into a shed or garage where it will be a few degrees warmer.

Maintenance
Repotting: Every one to two years in mid spring. Older and larger specimens every three years.

Use standard bonsai mix with an extra 20 percent grit.

Pruning: Prune branches, improve branch structure, and thin overgrown spurs in spring, three weeks after repotting. Seal all wounds immediately to keep out fungal spores, particularly coral spot which can attack live tissue on this species. Prune away unwanted adventitious shoots as soon as they appear.

Pinching: Pinching and trimming a large cotoneaster bonsai is almost a full-time occupation. Use sharp, pointed scissors to cut out all vigorous shoots completely. Other, less-vigorous shoots should be cut back to two or three leaves, which will gradually build up a network of short spurs. It is tempting to just trim the foliage like a hedge, but this "random pruning" does not allow you to control the growth pattern and structure of the branches, so resist temptation.

Watering: Cotoneasters are frequently used by gardeners to cover dry banks where little else will grow. In containers they are rather less happy in too-dry soil, but will suffer root rot if the soil is wet. Water only when the soil appears on the dry side in summer and keep the soil barely moist in winter. Shelter from persistent winter rain.

Feeding: Balanced food from spring until late summer, followed by nitrogen-free in early autumn.

Beware! Cotoneasters contain a toxin that is highly poisonous to some other plants. Clean tools thoroughly after use with methylated spirit.

Cryptomeria japonica
Japanese Cedar

Outdoor

Cryptomeria are tall, elegant trees with wide, shallow pads of foliage sitting on top of horizontal, fan-shaped branch structures. The needle-like leaves densely clothe the fleshy green shoots which curl downward when young, unable to support the weight of foliage. As the shoots mature, they stiffen and are held erect.

As a response to pruning and regular pinching, abundant adventitious shoots emerge from twig and branch intersections. These are used to replace old and congested twigs that are periodically thinned out.

Like all conifers, the *cryptomeria* branches are supple and bend easily – up to a point. If bent just a little too far they suddenly snap, so follow the guidelines in the section on *Carpinus* (see page 80). If a branch does snap during wiring, it won't break off entirely, but will remain attached by a sliver of bark and wood. Cut off the wire, reassemble the branch and bind it tightly with raffia, sealing the whole area with cut paste. The branch should survive but there will always be a weak point, so remember where the break was and avoid bending again at that point.

In winter the foliage changes color and adopts a bronze or brown tint. This looks at first as if the tree is dying, but it is a perfectly normal reaction to the change in season and is nothing to worry about. The foliage returns to its healthy green color as the weather improves in spring. This is the signal that it is time to repot.

It takes many years for a young cryptomeria to reach this stage of development, with all the branches neatly organized and trimmed, but it's worth the wait

Where to keep *cryptomeria*

In their native Japan, *cryptomeria* inhabit the lower slopes of mountains where they are shrouded in mist in the morning and exposed to the sun for the rest of the day. Provided you can ensure that the pot will not dry out through evaporation, and you can spray the foliage two or three times a day, your *cryptomeria* will do well in full sun. If you are not so confident, then try semi-shade, but ensure that the tree has good overhead light.

In winter you only need to protect *cryptomeria* from wind and prolonged periods of heavy frost.

Maintenance

Repotting: Repot younger trees every two years in mid spring. Older and larger specimens every five years. Use standard bonsai mix.

Pruning: Prune branches and improve branch structure in late summer while the tree still has time to begin healing before winter, but it is too late for adventitious growth. Thin out congested areas in spring and pull out all unwanted adventitious growth as soon as it appears.

Pinching: All new shoots should have their tips pinched out with the fingers while they are still soft and the needles are pale green. This is a weekly task that continues throughout the growing season.

Watering: Cryptomeria like cool, moist roots, so water well during the growing season but not so often that the soil is permanently saturated. In winter only water when the soil appears to be drying out.

Feeding: Balanced food from spring until late summer, followed by nitrogen-free in early autumn and a slow-release organic feed in mid-winter to nourish the spring growth.

Beware! The dense foliage of *cryptomeria* provides a haven for red spider mites which suck the sap from the fine shoots and the bases of leaves, causing large areas to turn brown and die back. Clean out all old foliage and spray daily with cold water and monthly with insecticide as a preventative measure.

Cycas Cycad

Cycads are among the most ancient species on earth, forming the link between ferns and trees in the evolutionary process. They are true tropicals that thrive on heat and humidity, and cannot cope with dry conditions. The first hint of dry roots will cause immediate loss of foliage and, quite likely, the plant will continue to deteriorate until it finally dies.

Although not trees in the strict sense, cycads can be enjoyable to grow as bonsai since they evoke images of tropical islands. To enhance this, try displaying your cycad by standing the pot in a shallow tray filled with pebbles kept moist.

When buying a cycad, check that the growing tip in the center of the rosette of fronds is green and healthy. Occasionally the growing tip will die if the plant is stressed, which inevitably leads to disappointment.

Where to keep cycads

The hotter and more humid the better as far as cycads are concerned. They will be happy in full sun outdoors in summer, provided they have been very carefully and gradually acclimatized, but changing their position is always a risky business. Indoors, the sun through glass is too intense – the humid atmosphere in their nat-ural habitat filters the sunlight – so provide some light shade such as an open-weave net curtain. Some cycad enthusiasts find that by placing their plants in a west-facing window, the need for shade is eliminated.

Maintenance

Repotting: Cycads are intolerant of excessive disturbance to the roots, which are thick and fleshy and very easily damaged, so be extremely careful when handling them. Normal root pruning is out of the question. Fortunately, they are extremely slow-growing so only need repotting every five years at the most. The best advice is to increase the size of the pot at each repotting without disturbing the roots at all. Use a cactus compost.

Pruning: Since there are no branches, conventional pruning does not apply. Dead fronds should be cut off – NOT pulled – close to the stem, with a sharp knife. Angle the cut so that it slopes downward away from the stem to produce the diamond-patterned texture familiar on the trunks of palm trees.

Pinching: Don't pinch out the growing tip at any time. At best this will distort the plant; at worst it might kill it.

Cycads can bring an air of sundrenched tropical islands into your home, especially welcome when the weather outside is cold and foggy

Watering: In winter the growth becomes slower, with the corresponding reduction in water uptake, so if the soil is already wet, there is no need to water. If the soil remains saturated for too long in winter it may become stagnant and emit an unpleasant smell.

Feeding: Feed gently with balanced fertilizer all year round, reducing the strength in winter. Mild foods such as fish emulsion can be used as directed; others should be used at half strength.

Beware! Cycads are extremely sensitive to changes in their local environment. After a sudden drop in local temperature, even by five degrees or so, the fronds will turn yellow and fall. Draft, reduction in humidity, reduced light levels and so on, will all have a similar effect. If this happens to your cycad, place it in a warm, bright location and keep the roots warm and slightly moist. Within a few weeks it should show signs of recovery.

Fagus crenata Japanese Beech

Varieties of beech are common woodland and parkland trees throughout temperate regions, but only the Japanese beech is used for commercial bonsai production. The smooth pale-gray bark persists throughout the tree's life, so the image of a mature tree can be established in a relatively young bonsai. When cleaned with an old toothbrush the bark can appear almost white, which contrasts particularly well with the copper-colored leaves in winter *(see below)*. The neat, slightly crinkly-edged, pointed leaves are borne on slender shoots which grow prolifically from dormant buds and old internodes.

In autumn the leaves on a bonsai that has been properly shaded during high summer will turn yellow before becoming coppery brown. If the tree has been exposed to too much sun the leaves will bypass the yellow phase. On young trees in the wild, the brown leaves remain on the tree all winter to protect the long, pointed buds from snow and birds, finally falling as the buds begin to open in spring. All bonsai, regardless of their actual age, are horticulturally "young," so your

beech should keep its leaves all winter too.

If you want to remove these leaves during the winter in order to wire-train the branches, cut through the petioles rather than attempt to pull the leaves away, which would risk causing damage to the delicate buds.

Where to keep beeches

Beeches can be kept in full sun for much of the time, but in summer the sun may cause the leaves to become paler than normal and adopt a hard, leathery surface which renders them less efficient at manufacturing essential sugars. Provide some shade during the hottest part of the year and return the tree to full sun as autumn approaches.

Beeches tolerate freezing well and only need to be brought into a shed or garage if temperatures threaten to remain below 12.6°F (-7°C) for more than a week.

Maintenance

Repotting: Every two to three years in spring. You can repot in autumn provided you can keep the tree more or less frost-free until spring – minimum -2°C. (3.6°F.).

Use standard soil or Akadama. If using Akadama, be especially vigilant with watering during the first three months while new roots are being established.

Pruning: Prune the branches in late winter or early spring, three weeks

Beech are sturdy trees with pale gray bark and copper-colored autumn foliage which remains on the tree until spring to protect the buds

before or after repotting. Pruning in mid-summer will encourage vigorous regeneration from around the wound.

Pinching: Pinch out the growing tips once two true leaves have begun to harden. Alternatively, to build up vigor in weak areas, allow the shoots to extend for six or seven leaves and then cut back to two.

Watering: Water well during the growing season and keep moist in winter. In really hot weather water twice a day as necessary.

Feeding: Balanced food during the growing season, nitrogen-free food in late

summer and autumn. Delay the first spring feed until three weeks after the buds have opened.

Beware! Beech leaves scorch easily when exposed to drying winds and can become pale and inefficient in strong sun. Although full-sized trees can tolerate both these conditions to a certain extent, trees in containers cannot. Protect from wind and sun at all times.

Ficus Fig

Outdoor

The varieties of fig used for bonsai cultivation in China, Taiwan, and Korea are closely related to the "rubber plant" which is an almost mandatory house-plant in the west. *Ficus retusa* and *Ficus benjamina* are both native to south-east Asia and are jungle plants. *Ficus microphylla* (small-leaved) come from Australia and inhabit more exposed areas.

The one thing all figs have in common is their habit of producing aerial roots from branches and the upper trunk. In nature, the aerial roots growing from the branches eventually become strong enough to support the parent branch both structurally and nutritionally. Those emerging from the trunk tend to self-graft to the trunk as they grow down-ward. This causes the trunk to thicken rapidly and adopt a deeply fluted appearance.

Large specimen bonsai figs use this natural process to good effect, but smaller ones are not vigorous enough for the self-grafting process to take place. If you want to develop your fig into a larger specimen, plant it in a bigger container – the bigger the better, and keep it in a warm, bright, and humid position. Feed well and allow all shoots to grow to about ten leaves before hard-pruning to leave just one or two leaves. After four or five years you should have built up a plant that is large enough for the aerial roots to self-graft when it is replanted into a larger bonsai pot.

The roots of *ficus* varieties are thick and fleshy, and quickly bond together when allowed to touch. This characteristic is often used to good effect, as with this interesting specimen

Where to keep figs

Although in nature many figs grow in full sun, most are ideally suited to life in the dappled shade of taller trees with sparse foliage, where their roots are in cooler, humus-rich soil and the surrounding air is humid. Keep your figs in good light but protected from direct sun, even if placed outdoors in summer.

Moving figs from one room to another or expos-ing them to drafts or dry air can cause the older leaves to turn yellow and fall. So once you have found a position that suits your bonsai, leave it there permanently, turning it around once a week to ensure that it receives an even amount of light on all sides.

Maintenance

Repotting: Every two to three years in winter, or at any other time of year with care. Keep the pot warm after root-pruning to encourage the rapid regen-eration of roots, and never water right after repotting or all the leaves will drop. Use standard soil.

Pruning: Prune in winter when the sap flow is reduced. Figs "bleed" a milky sap profusely from pruning wounds at all times of the year. Figs respond well to hard-prun-ing and will throw out new shoots from all parts of the tree.

Pinching: Pinch out the growing tips once two true leaves form.

Watering: Water well during the growing season and keep moist in winter. In really hot weather water trees in very shallow con-tainers twice a day as necessary.

Feeding: Balanced food during the growing season, reduced to half-strength in winter.

Beware! The bark on most *ficus* varieties swells rapidly when the plant is growing and is being well-watered. This can cause wire to make scars within a few weeks. Check all wire regu-larly and remove it as soon as it appears too tight, reapplying it afterward if necessary.

Ginkgo biloba
Ginkgo

Outdoor

Ginkgos are curious trees. They are the oldest of all trees alive today and are closely related to ferns. Once thought to be extinct, they were rediscovered in China in the 17th Century and are now planted as street trees throughout the world.

The natural shape of the ginkgo is tall and columnar. The trunks and branches become quite gnarled with age, but never develop a refined structure. They also resent pruning. Frequently pruned shoots will die back, sometimes right back to the parent branch. A branch with many pruned shoots may, in turn, die back to the trunk. In bonsai, the treatment aims at producing a characterful trunk onto which sufficient foliage-bearing shoots will grow each year to nourish the plant. To minimize the die-back, leave a short stub and seal it immediately.

Ginkgos naturally form tall, conical trees which become gnarled and twisted with age. This bonsai is already beginning to display the same character

Ginkgos have a habit of growing vigorously one year and hardly at all the next. They also tend to abort some shoots during the winter, which makes serious attempts at wire-training futile. For this reason, ginkgo are generally grown for their vivid yellow autumn color and not for their shape.

Mature ginkgo bonsai are little more than gnarled stumps with short, stubby branches bearing equally short shoots which are replaced every year or so by new ones.

Where to keep ginkgos

Ginkgos are happy either in full sun or partial shade. Sun will improve autumn color, but if the soil is allowed to dry out through evaporation the tree will respond by aborting shoots and branches. Shade prevents this but tends to encourage leggy growth and large leaves. If you are serious about keeping a ginkgo bonsai, be prepared for several years of trial and error – particularly error – until you find the right location or combination of locations that suit your particular tree in your garden.

Protection from all but light frost is mandatory. Never bring a ginkgo into the house in winter.

Maintenance

Repotting: Every year in late winter or early spring. Use very sharp tools to avoid crushing the fleshy roots. Use standard soil with a little extra moisture-retentive organic matter.

Pruning: Prune branches and old shoots in late spring, three or more weeks after repotting, when the swelling buds will indicate which shoots have survived the winter. If you prune in autumn or winter you may remove viable shoots and leave those which are already destined to abort.

Pinching: Pinch out the growing tips once two true leaves form.

Watering: Water well during the growing season and keep barely moist in winter. Spray foliage regularly.

Feeding: Balanced food during the growing season, nitrogen-free in autumn.

Beware! The thick fleshy roots of ginkgos contain a large quantity of water which expands on freezing and can burst the roots like a frozen water pipe. This is especially dangerous when there is an imbalance of moisture between the roots and the surrounding soil. It is wiser to protect your ginkgo from prolonged or severe freezing than to try to maintain moisture balance all winter.

Ilex crenata
Japanese Holly

Indoor & Outdoor

Ironically the Japanese call this charming tree "English holly," but it could hardly be more distinct from holly. To begin with, it is deciduous. Its tiny oval leaves have no sharp spines and they turn anything from yellow, through orange, to red in autumn. Although the flowers are insignificant and easy to miss unless you look closely, if fertilized by a nearby male tree, they will produce masses of small red berries which

can remain on the tree until the following spring if the birds don't get them first.

The bark is comparatively thick and fleshy, so wiring must be done with great care. If you wire when the soil is on the dry side, the branches – which are rather brittle – will bend a little more easily and the bark is less likely to be damaged. However, since Japanese holly grows slowly, it may take a year or two for the branches to set in position. Check regularly that the wire is not scarring the bark as it swells, especially at the top of the tree. As soon as the wire appears too tight remove it and reapply it, coiling in the opposite direction.

The colorful berries of Japanese holly delight the birds as well as the eye! If you want to enjoy your bonsai in fruit, keep it under bird netting from late summer onward

Where to keep *Ilex crenata*

Keep it wherever you like! Japanese holly is one of the very few species that can be kept indoors or outdoors, and in sun or shade. It requires a dormant period in winter, but that need not involve sub-zero temperatures. Moving your ilex into an unheated room will suffice. In summer it will appreciate some fresh air through an open window and a misting with cool water two or three times a day.

Outdoors, if kept in sun, your only worry will be that the roots don't dry out, which is the one thing that *Ilex crenata* do not tolerate. The growth will be slower and the leaves smaller on trees exposed to the sun. In shade the shoots extend further and the leaves are a little larger, but remain in better condition. Autumn color is improved by placing the tree in shade during summer and acclimatizing it to the sun in early autumn.

Maintenance

Repotting: Every two to three years in late winter or early spring. Use standard soil or Japanese Akadama.

Pruning: Prune branches and old shoots in late spring, before the buds have opened. Alternatively, prune in autumn and keep the tree frost-free all winter. Hollow out wounds to prevent the healing tissues from forming unsightly swelling. Hard-prune in summer to regenerate vigorous growth on weak branches.

Pinching: Pinch out the growing tips once flowering is over, and trim lightly to shape as necessary throughout the rest of the growing season.

Watering: Water well during the growing season and keep barely moist in winter. Spray foliage regularly in warm weather.

Feeding: Balanced food during the growing season, nitrogen-free in autumn.

Beware! When you see a Japanese holly covered with berries in the nursery, it is a female tree. Don't be misled into thinking that it will be covered in fruit again next year, because unless you buy a male tree to accompany it, you will be disappointed. The fruit will only set if the flower has been fertilized and there are few, if any, *Ilex crenata* in gardens to do the job.

Juniperus chinensis
Chinese Juniper

Outdoor

In the mountains of Japan these tough trees adopt gnarled and twisted trunks and branches with large areas of exposed "driftwood"; this habit is generally echoed in bonsai. Provided you leave sufficient foliage to sustain the plant, you have total creative freedom in making your own jins and sharis to improve or even entirely redesign your bonsai.

The densely borne shoots rapidly form a neat, clearly defined silhouette with regular pinching. Periodically, the foliage

should be thinned out and the silhouette rebuilt with younger shoots that constantly emerge from branch intersections in healthy plants. The outer bark, which is gray-brown and flaky, can be carefully peeled off to reveal the smooth orange-red underbark which contrasts beautifully with the rich green foliage and the silvery-white jins and sharis.

Juniper branches are notoriously slow to set after wiring. The springy, resinous nature of the heartwood, the relatively thin layers of xylem deposited each year, and their unusual longevity

Chinese junipers can be shaped to almost any style. This superb cascade style depicts a tree clinging to life on a mountain ledge

combine to make juniper bonsai the most time-consuming of all. Young branches, up to ¼ in. (5 mm) thick on young trees, may set in a year or two, but older branches, especially on older trees, may never set. It is common to see masterpiece juniper bonsai exhibited in Japan with every branch wired from trunk to tip.

Where to keep Chinese juniper

Junipers do well in full sun, producing neat, compact foliage. If placed in semi-shade the growth will be slower to start in spring but the color will be somewhat richer.

There is no need to protect your juniper from frost, but the cold wind may cause the foliage to turn bronze. Don't be too concerned if this happens; it will turn green again in spring.

Maintenance

Repotting: Every two to five years in mid spring. Use standard soil with an additional 20 percent finely chopped fresh sphagnum moss (the kind used to line hanging baskets).

Pruning: Prune branches and old shoots in late summer when the sap is not rising too fast and "bleeding" is less of a problem, and there is still time for the wound to heal before winter.

Pinching: Pinch out all the growing tips with the fingers to keep a neat silhouette. Vigorous extension shoots should be cut back as far as possible to a healthy side shoot or removed completely. Clean all foliage from the undersides of the branches.

Watering: Water well during the growing season and keep barely moist in winter. Although junipers are drought-tolerant, they can consume a surprising amount of water when it is available, especially during winter.

Feeding: Balanced food during the growing season, nitrogen-free in autumn. An additional dose of slow-release balanced food in mid-winter will strengthen spring growth.

Beware! In the wild junipers naturally shed branches from time to time in order to maintain a balance between the efficiency of the roots and the demand of the foliage. This also happens with container-grown plants, so if a branch dies on your juniper it is probably not your fault.

Juniperus rigida
Needle Juniper

Needle junipers are aptly named. The first thing you learn about them is that the needle-like leaves, borne in groups of three, are very sharp and take some getting used to! They can also be temperamental – losing shoots or branches, refusing to grow where you expect them to, and so on. However, once established and growing well, needle junipers are one of the finest species for bonsai and good examples are much sought after by the connoisseur.

The young shoots are flaccid and droop downward, temporarily giving the tree an untidy appearance. As they mature they strengthen and hold themselves more upright, but they should be pinched back before they reach that stage. At the base of each needle is a tiny embryonic bud which has the potential to grow into a new shoot. Light pinching will induce the two or three buds nearest to the tip to extend; harder pinching will induce a greater number of buds to extend and more adventitious shoots to emerge from two- or three-year-old wood.

It is essential to thin out congested areas of foliage every few years to allow light and air into the center of the tree. Cut out old, woody spurs, leaving intact the fresh new growth from further down the branch. This will then be used to rebuild the foliage clouds.

Where to keep needle juniper

Needle junipers thrive in full sun. If they are grown in shade the shoots become leggy, unable to support their own weight, and prone to die-back. Place another bonsai or some other object close to the pot to shade the roots from the hot sun during mid-summer.

In winter protect from prolonged or severe freezing to stop the foliage from turning brown and to ensure that the roots do not suffer. By the time you are aware of a problem with the roots, it may be too late to remedy it.

The deadwood on this needle juniper already existed when it was gathered from the wild. The final image is that of a much taller conifer standing alone on a remote mountainside

Maintenance

Repotting: Every two to five years in mid spring. Use standard soil with an additional 20 percent grit, or Akadama.

Pruning: Prune branches in late spring, but not in the same year as repotting. Use the stubs of pruned branches to shape into jins, or consider linking two jins with a shari *(see page 69).* Thin out congested areas in summer.

Pinching: Pinch out all the growing tips with the fingers to keep a neat silhouette. Vigorous extension shoots should be cut back to three or four needles. Clean all foliage from the undersides of the branches.

Watering: Water well during the growing season and keep barely moist in winter. Avoid waterlogged soil at all costs.

Feeding: Half-strength balanced food during the growing season, nitrogen-free in autumn. An additional dose of slow-release balanced food at half-strength in mid-winter will strengthen spring growth.

Beware! Needle junipers have a reputation for dying without any apparent cause. The truth is that there is always a cause but the metabolism of this species is so slow that a plant can be dead for a year or more before the foliage starts to dry off and the shoots stop extending.

The smooth bark of this crape myrtle will soon begin to flake away, revealing an ever-changing pattern of pinks and browns. With luck, it will also provide its owner with a flush of vivid flowers in late summer

Lagerstroemia Crape Myrtle

Originally from China and Korea, where all commercial bonsai are produced, crape myrtles have now become popular garden and hedging plants in Mediterranean and sub-tropical regions throughout the world. They are grown mainly for their short-lived but flamboyant late summer or early autumn display of flowers, which vary from shades of lilac, through pinks, to almost white. In bonsai culture, however, the plant can sometimes be reluctant to flower, since efficient flowering depends on so many elements that are all provided by the owner, who doesn't always get it right!

However, the bark of crape myrtle is sufficiently striking to make it a worth-while species for bonsai even without the flowers. As the bark ages it peels away in irregular flakes, revealing a different-colored under-bark. This can vary from pale gray through shades of rust and brown to almost pink, depending on the time of year. This constantly changing tapestry of color provides year-round interest and a charm that is found in very few other species, and can occur on relatively young plants. Spraying regularly with fresh water and exposure to the sun will encourage the bark to flake.

Where to keep crape myrtle

Full sun in summer, either close to an open window or outside on a balcony or window sill. Crape myrtle will tolerate sun through glass without any serious side-effects. If leaving the tree outside at night, acclimatize it first by gradually increasing the length of time spent outside each day. Choose a mild night for the tree's first night out.

In winter reduce light levels as well as temperature to induce dormancy. Insufficient dormancy will induce premature spring growth and weaken the tree. It will also either shorten the already-brief flowering period or eliminate it for a year.

Maintenance

Repotting: Every one to three years in mid spring. Use standard bonsai soil.

Pruning: Prune branches in autumn, hollowing out the wound to prevent swelling as it heals. Allow spring growth to extend until the leaves begin to harden and cut all shoots back to two or three leaves. The next crop of shoots will bear the flowers in late summer/autumn, and should not be trimmed until you are sure where the flower buds have formed.

Pinching: You must decide whether you want a year-round neat tree or flowers *(see above)*. If you want flowers, don't pinch out any growth until late summer when the flower buds will be visible and can be left on the plant. Pinch over-extended shoots only to keep the tree reasonably neat at this time.

Watering: Water well during the growing season and sparingly when the tree is dormant. The swelling of the buds in spring will tell you that it is time to gradually increase the water.

Feeding: To maximize flowering and to keep vigor under control, give regular low-nitrogen feeds throughout the growing period and one or two doses of nitrogen-free food in autumn.

Beware! Lagerstroemia must have a dormant period each winter in order to thrive. During this time temperatures must be kept between 41-50°F (7-10°C), and light and water kept to the bare minimum.

Ligustrum sinensis Chinese Privet

Indoor & Outdoor

Privet hedging, *Ligustrum ovalifolium*, is common throughout the Mediterranean and temperate zones of the world. Its dark-green foliage and dusty interior, combined with its ability to prevent any other plants, apart from rank weeds, from growing close to it, has earned privet a reputation of being a somewhat vulgar species and not one which would normally be associated with beautiful bonsai.

All privets make excellent bonsai. Their glossy oval leaves are borne in pairs on straight shoots, which emerge prolifically from young and old wood alike in response to pruning and pinching. They are strong growers and thrive in poor soils, requiring little in the way of nutrients. Although classed as evergreens, in temperate climates they become semi-evergreen. In very cold winters the foliage turns purple and some or all of the leaves may be shed, depending on the temperature and situation. This can be quite startling the first time it happens, but when spring arrives the plant always bounces back with a new crop of vigorous new shoots.

Where to keep privet

Chinese privet is extremely tough and versatile and is one of the few species that is equally at home in a centrally heated house or out in the garden or back yard. If grown indoors it will need as much light as possible all year round, but outside privet will grow happily in sun or shade. However, when grown in shade the leaves will be larger and more lush in color and texture. They will also be more likely to fall in winter.

Maintenance

Repotting: Every two to four years in mid spring. Privet can be repotted as late as mid-summer if root disturbance is kept to a minimum.

Use standard bonsai soil or Akadama.

Pruning: Prune branches late spring or early summer. Thin out congested spurs in mid-summer and wire-train all new shoots while they are still green.

Pinching: Large specimen bonsai can be allowed to grow unpinched from early summer onward to maximize flowering. Smaller bonsai will look far too untidy, so it is best to sacrifice the flowers and pinch back all new growth as necessary to keep the tree neat.

Watering: Maintain even moisture in the soil throughout the year and *never* overwater. Dry soil can become difficult to re-wet, particularly if the organic matter used is peat-based. Dry roots will cause lower branches to die back. Every two or three weeks, immerse the pot in a bowl of water so the water is at the same level as the surface of the soil. When the surface of the soil appears wet, remove the pot from the bowl and drain it thoroughly.

Feeding: To keep vigor under control and to induce flowering, feed with low-nitrogen fertilizer throughout the growing season. A single dose of nitrogen-free food in autumn will toughen plants kept outside.

Beware! Ligustrum cannot tolerate having dry roots for several days (although it is not advisable to allow it to dry out intentionally, or too often) but the roots will soon start to decay if conditions are too wet. The pot also rapidly fills with dense fibrous roots which can make water penetration slow.

Malus spp.
Crab apple

There are countless varieties of crab apple used for bonsai, with blooms ranging from deep cerise, through shades of pink, to almost pure white. On some, the flowers are followed by fruit which can vary in size from ¼-1 ¼ in. (5–30 mm); on others fruiting is rare or inconsistent. However, the fruit is of secondary importance to the flowers and it is good practice to remove the fruit anyway, to divert more energy into producing next year's flower buds.

Varieties of *malus* are invariably grafted onto dwarfing root stocks because they tend to be inefficient when growing on their own roots. Sometimes the graft union swells or leaves an obvious scar which will disfigure the tree and gets worse as the tree ages. Bearing this in mind, take extra care when buying crab apple bonsai.

Where to keep crab apples

In spite of their delicate beauty, crab apples are among the toughest and most hardy of all species used for bonsai. They adore sunshine, but perform disappointingly when grown in shade. In winter they can tolerate heavy freezing for long periods and only need to be protected from really severe freezing to make you feel more comfortable – not the tree! Having said that, small bonsai in small containers may be slightly more at risk in really bad winters.

Bring your crab apple indoors in spring for a day or so to admire the flowers, but return it to the outside at night.

Maintenance

Repotting: Every one to two years in autumn. Can be repotted in early spring, but this may result in poor flowering. Use a deeper than normal pot. Use standard bonsai soil with an additional 20 percent organic matter or some granular clay-based soil.

Pruning: Prune branches late spring, after flowering. Also at this time prune all of last year's shoots that have not flowered back to a short stub. Once the shape of the tree is established, maximize flowering by allowing all new growth to extend until mid- to late-summer, by which time the growth should have more or less ceased and the fat flower buds will be visible at the base of the shoots. Cut back all shoots to leave two to four of these buds.

Pinching: Avoid pinching during the first part of the summer as you may be restricting the growth of shoots that would bear flower buds at the base if left alone. Pinching will encourage vegetative growth at the expense of flower production. Only pinch out the tips of any over-extending shoots that are produced in response to the late summer pruning.

Watering: Water well during the growing season, particularly while the fruit is being formed, because the fruit contains over 80 percent water. Keep moist but not wet in winter. Spray foliage and flowers regularly with fresh water.

Feeding: Balanced food in spring, when flowering is over, followed by low-nitrogen in summer and nitrogen-free in autumn. Feed generously, but take care not to exceed the manufacturer's instructions. Half-strength administered twice as often is ideal.

Beware! Crab apples prefer a deeper pot than most species to ensure there is always an adequate supply of moisture and nutrients. The strain of such prolific flowering and fruiting can drain a tree and if the pot is not deep enough, loss of some branches may occur.

Below: Crab apple bonsai are pruned in late summer to induce prolific flowering the following spring

Right: Delicate crab apple blossom can vary from almost pure white through to deep pink

Although *Murraya* are not the easiest of species to keep indoors, the interesting bark textures and vigorous growth make the extra effort worthwhile

Murraya paniculata
Jasmine Orange

Indoor

The fragrant white flowers and small orange fruit earned this native of India its common name, although it is not related to either jasmine or the citrus family.

It has small compound leaves which are held on stiff stems and produces new shoots from old wood after pruning. The bark is smooth and pale gray-brown when young, displaying more gray and breaking into fine vertical ridges as it ages. In spite of jasmine orange's readiness to produce adventitious shoots, the canopy seldom becomes as dense as other broad leaved species. The compound leaves are specifically designed to keep the canopy open and less vulnerable to damage by tropical winds.

For best results, spray your *murraya* regularly with fresh water and stand the pot in a tray of water, supported on stones to keep the drainage holes clear of the surface. This will increase local humidity and simulate the tree's natural habitat.

Where to keep jasmine orange

Jasmine orange is a true tropical that thrives in hot, steamy forests where there is ample rainfall and the temperature rarely falls below 62.6°F (17°C). Most homes have a room that can provide these conditions for most of the time, but it is not quite so easy to maintain jungle-like conditions all year round. A reduction of temperature or light will slow or halt growth for a period, which is not a problem if it only happens once a year. But if the tree's local environment is allowed to vary too often its health will deteriorate.

A sunny window sill in a kitchen or heated bathroom would be perfect, provided the window is not opened during the colder months. The sudden appearance of even a slightly cool breeze will cause the loss of large areas of foliage and some young shoots.

Maintenance

Repotting: Every two to four years in spring. Keep the pot warm after repotting to aid regeneration of the roots. Use standard bonsai soil with an additional 30 percent organic matter or granular clay-based soil.

Pruning: Prune branches hard in December and seal wounds immediately to prevent further die-back. If die-back occurs, incorporate it into the design of the bonsai by creating interesting hollows. Prevent further decay by treating the exposed wood with lime-sulphur solution that has a little India ink added to tone down the color.

Pinching: Once the silhouette of the foliage clouds has been established, simply pinch out the growing tips of all extending shoots, leaving two or three leaves intact. Clean out dead twigs from time to time.

Watering: Water well while the tree is in active growth and reduce water slightly when growth slows down in winter. Never let the soil become dry. Immerse the pot in a bowl of water once a week to ensure there are no hidden dry spots in the center of the root ball. Spraying may cause the bark to swell and fall away.

Feeding: Half-strength balanced food throughout the year, provided the tree is in active growth. Withhold food if growth ceases during the winter.

Beware! The bark on *murraya* is quite thick and separates easily from the heartwood if handled carelessly. Too much pressure when wiring, or the use of blunt tools which crush rather than cut when pruning, will result in disaster. Watch out for mildew on plants subjected to poor air circulation, and aphids on all plants.

Myrtus apiculata Myrtle

Indoor

One of the most popular subjects for bonsai in China, *myrtus* indeed offers the bonsai enthusiast an opportunity to create a fine specimen in a relatively short time, with its vigorous growth, small shiny leaves and beautiful, tiny white flowers with golden centers.

Most commercial myrtle bonsai are produced in vast numbers in China, Taiwan, and Korea, and tend to be modest both in size and quality. However, they do constitute excellent material to develop further. Occasionally, larger, more refined specimens appear in nurseries. These are usually developed from wild or field-grown material and are well worth the additional expense.

When buying myrtle bonsai, check that the roots have not deteriorated due to overwatering in the nursery. Gently rock the tree in its pot – if it feels a little unstable, don't buy it.

Where to keep myrtle

Myrtles are sub-tropicals so they require warmth throughout the year, but with slightly reduced temperatures in winter so the tree can enter its semi-dormant rest period. In fact, in summer it cannot be too hot for myrtles. They adore heat and relatively high humidity, but are not as happy if exposed to direct sun through glass.

If kept indoors all year round, place near a sunny window but where it will be shaded from afternoon sun. Outdoors in summer, the tree can be exposed to full sun, but the pot should be shaded to prevent the roots from overheating.

In winter maintain temperatures at about 41-46°F (5-7°C) and keep away from cold drafts.

Maintenance

Repotting: Every two to three years in spring. Take care not to cut too far into old roots. If you want to reduce the heavier roots, do so over a number of years.

Use standard bonsai mix, using ericaceous (lime-free) compost for the organic content. Myrtles sometimes lose their leaves after root pruning, and they can take a long time to regrow, so be patient.

Pruning: You can prune your myrtle at any time of year, but it is best done while the tree is resting. Pruning while the tree is growing will encourage the production of masses of unwanted adventitious shoots.

Pinching: The prolific slender shoots are too numer-

Myrtles produce an abundance of shoots and flowers, making them ideal subjects for bonsai and as popular in the West as they are in their native China

ous for handpinching to be practical, so use sharp nail scissors to trim the foliage clouds to shape whenever the tree looks untidy. Myrtles produce hundreds of adventitious shoots from all parts of the branches and trunk. These must be painstakingly removed by pulling them away cleanly. If you try to cut these off you will leave a short stub from which many more shoots will rapidly appear.

Watering: Water carefully during the growing period, keeping the soil moist but never allowing it to become saturated. Myrtles dislike having their roots wet for too long. In winter keep the watering to a minimum – just enough to prevent the

soil from becoming completely dry. Spray with fresh water daily.

Feeding: Half-strength balanced food while the tree is in active growth. Do not feed in winter when the growth slows to a standstill.

Beware! Myrtles are "calcifuges" – lime-haters – and will slowly deteriorate if constantly supplied with hard tapwater. The leaves will begin to turn yellow and will soon fall, causing die-back of young shoots as the lime builds up around the roots and "locks" nutrients in the soil. Use collected rainwater whenever possible and treat with a proprietary soil acidifier three or four times a year.

Nandina domestica
Sacred Bamboo

This is another species whose common name is misleading. *Nandina* is neither a bamboo nor particularly sacred. It is, however, an attractive subject for cultivation in shallow containers. It has bamboo-like leaves which emerge deep red and often remain that color for several months, particularly in good light. The small, whitish flowers are borne in loose spikes and are followed by bright red berries. Its habit of producing a multitude of new shoots from ground level means that it is particularly difficult to create a trunk

of any worth, so the ideal style for this species is a clump or grove.

After a number of years the base may become woody, and it can then be exposed by raising the plant in its pot. Constant hard-pruning of old stems will eventually add much character and interest.

Alternatively, you can encourage the clump to spread sideways by selective pruning and division at repotting time. In this way you will eventually create an image of a bamboo grove.

Where to keep *nandinas*

Nandinas are happy to spend all year in most normal domestic environments, provided air circulation is good and there

Nandina are similar to bamboo although they are not related in any way. The leaves adopt a beautiful rich red color when kept in good light

is sufficient light, but not in direct sunlight at any time. However, they will benefit from being allowed to spend the warmer months outside in semi-shade, where the summer breeze causes the slender stems to sway and the night-time dew keeps the foliage fresh. If kept indoors in summer, place near an open window to ensure good air circulation and spray twice a day with fresh water.

Nandinas must not be subjected to temperatures below 44.6°F (7°C) at any time. The foliage and stems are able to withstand lower temperatures but the roots are not.

Maintenance

Repotting: Every three to four years in spring. Clumps can be divided at repotting time, either to create additional plantings or to increase the size of the existing one by spreading out the segments in a larger container. Use standard bonsai soil with an additional 30 percent organic matter to increase moisture retention.

Pruning: Prune old stems right back, either to ground level or to the old, woody, stump-like base. Many new shoots will emerge as a result and these should be thinned to prevent overcrowding and to maintain an elegant composition.

Pinching: Snip off the tips of side shoots to maintain an overall neat appearance. Take care not to trim off the flowering shoots which usually emerge in early summer from a near-apical bud on last year's growth.

Watering: Nandina naturally grows in areas where the soil is permanently moist, such as woodland margins and sheltered valleys. Keep the soil moist at all times but avoid waterlogging.

Feeding: Low-nitrogen fertilizer throughout the growing period. Excess nitrogen causes leggy stems and oversized leaves.

Beware! Young *nandinas* are not strong and are less resilient than older examples. The shock of transportation from the Far East and the consequent change of growing conditions can seriously damage a young plant. Avoid small *nandinas* that display any sign of weakness or die-back. It is better to pay a little extra for a more sturdy specimen that has been in the country for several months and has had time to recover from the trauma.

Olea europea
Olive

Indoor

Olives are one of the few species used commercially for bonsai production in Europe. They are propagated by the thousands in Italy, Spain, and Israel – the latter supplying the Christmas gift market with tiny rooted cuttings. Olives can be easily transplanted even when very old. It is common practice for landscape gardeners in Mediterranean countries to transplant wild trees many centuries old. This remarkable property of olives enables commercial bonsai producers to collect wild material of considerable size and age and, as a result, some very fine specimen bonsai are now becoming available at reasonable cost.

Although olives are slow-growing, the shoots can extend rapidly in spring and again in early autumn. The plant's natural habit is to shut down during high summer when, in its natural habitat, it is too hot and dry for growth to take place. The white shoots are very rigid and grow in all directions. If you want to wire them, do so while they are still growing and have not yet become too brittle.

Where to keep trident olives

Olives prefer full sun all day, every day. They are extremely drought-tolerant so you don't need to worry too much if the heat of the sun completely dries out the soil from time to time. You will notice that after the soil has dried out the leaves will exude white resin as a means of preventing further evaporation of moisture through the pores. When watered after drought, olives consume vast amounts of water to be stored in the fleshy leaves and bark.

Although some strains of olive are claimed to be half-hardy and, indeed, survive frost and even snow in the wild, they should be considered as tender when grown in containers. Protect from temperatures below 41°F (5°C).

Maintenance

Repotting: Every three years or so – olives can live happily without repotting for up to a decade, but it is good practice to repot fairly regularly so you can inspect the general health of the plant. Use a mix of 30 percent organic matter to 70 percent grit.

Pruning: Prune in early autumn or early spring using a fine-toothed saw to cope with the extremely hard wood.

Warning: Olives do not regenerate new growth from immediately behind the wound on shortened branches. The stubs of shortened branches invariably die right back to their point of origin, and any new growth stimulated by the

Olives have only recently been developed as subjects for commercial bonsai production, so mature specimens are very rare. However, charming young bonsai like this are rapidly becoming popular

pruning will emerge from the trunk or the parent branch. To avoid disappointment, shorten branches in stages, saving the final cut until there are conveniently placed sideshoots to prune back to.

Pinching: The shoots are too tough for effective finger-pinching, so use sharp nail scissors to trim wayward shoots back to two or three leaves.

Watering: Keep the soil just moist enough to sustain the plant by watering heavily but infrequently, more infrequently in winter. Spray with fresh water in very hot weather.

Feeding: Half-strength solution of balanced food throughout summer and one nitrogen-free feed in autumn. Do not feed in winter, even if the plant appears to be growing.

Beware! Olive branches may be the symbol of peace, but they are annoyingly short-tempered in that they have little tolerance for bending and snap at the base very easily. Even if they don't snap they will often die back after wiring. However, new shoots grow in all directions and it is normally possible to shape a branch by selective pruning alone.

Pinus parviflora
Pinus pentaphylla)
White Pine

Outdoor

Japanese white pines live high in the rugged mountains where they battle for survival against the most severe conditions yet, surprisingly, they are the most dainty and elegant of all pines. Their small needles, borne in groups of five, are triangular in cross-section and are green on the underside and have silvery white lines along the centers of the other two sides, which gives the impression of the tree being bathed in a pale blue haze.

The bark on white pines remains smooth until the tree is very old so, in order to add interest and character, commercial bonsai are invariably grafted onto black pine trunks, which develop deep fissures much sooner. The graft is made immediately below the lowest branch so the foliage covers the rather obvious change in bark texture. If you are lucky enough to spot an ungrafted white pine with flaky bark right to the apex, snap it up – they are rare and highly prized.

On established bonsai, the old needles should be pulled out in late summer, first to allow light and air into the branches to strengthen inner growth and, second, to control the distribution of energy to different parts of the tree. Pull out more needles on the upper, more vigorous shoots, leaving four or five clusters intact. Increase the number of needles remaining to seven or eight clusters in the center of the tree, and ten or more on the lower branches. On the weakest branches of all, just clean out dead or dying needles. This process ensures that the tree's energy is not concentrated in the apex.

Where to keep white pines

White pines are designed to spend their summers in full sun and fresh air, so they only tolerate being indoors for a day or so at a time. In semi-shade the foliage loses much of its silvery sheen. In winter you only need to protect your white pine from persistent temperatures below 9°F (-5°C) and, of course, cold winds.

Maintenance

Repotting: Every two to five years in late spring. Be careful not to tear at the roots when you untangle them. If you see a white fluffy substance around the roots, you're in luck! This is a beneficial mycorrhyzal fungus that helps the tree digest nutrients. Root aphids also appear white and fluffy, but they move!

The blue-green needles of white pine are borne in closely-set groups of five, giving even a young plant a dense canopy. This older specimen boasts a long, sweeping lower branch, typical of trees growing on lower mountain slopes

Use a mix of 30 percent organic matter to 70 percent grit, or Akadama with 20 percent grit added.

Pruning: Prune in late summer to early autumn when the wounds are less likely to bleed resin, which stains the bark white. Seal wounds immediately.

Pinching: Break off the tips of the new shoots as they extend (see page 62 for detailed information on pinching pines).

Watering: Keep the soil moist but try never to saturate it. Pines prefer very free-draining soil so, to be safe, it is best to shelter them from prolonged rainfall.

Feeding: Half-strength solution of balanced food throughout summer and one nitrogen-free feed in autumn, plus a single application of slow-release organic fertilizer in mid-winter.

Beware! White pines are reluctant to produce adventitious buds on older wood, without which the branches could not be restructured periodically. Regular feeding, needle-pulling, and shoot-pinching is essential. When you do spot an adventitious bud, treasure it and wait a year or so before asking it to replace an older part of the branch which you want to prune away.

Pinus thunbergii
Japanese Black Pine

Outdoor

Pinus thunbergii are common parkland trees in their native Japan. Their tolerance of poor, dry soils and harsh pruning make them suitable even for planting in the centers of highway intersections and in busy city streets. They are even seen growing in the crevices between the walls of adjacent houses.

The needles are shiny, rich green and stand erect in pairs from the stout shoots. The charcoal-gray bark develops deep fissures in quite young trees and the branches thicken and mature in a relatively short time. Together these produce a strong, masculine tree, full of rugged character.

The needles are, if anything, a little longer than would be ideal. With strong, healthy trees, the water can be reduced to absolute minimum at the point in late spring when the needles are about half-size and beginning to stand away from the elongating "candle." This will arrest the development of the needles. Once the needles have hardened and are standing erect from the shoot, normal watering can be resumed and the needles will not extend. This routine can be repeated in alternate years.

Where to keep black pines

Black pines are designed to spend their summers in full sun and fresh air, so they only tolerate being indoors for a day or so at a time, and never in winter. In semi-shade the growth is weak and budding is poor. In winter you only need to protect your black pine from persistent temperatures below 9°F (-5°C), excessive rain, and cold winds.

Japanese black pines are strong trees with dark, craggy bark and bright green needles. This ancient specimen has a superbly-shaped trunk and excellent branch structure

Maintenance

Repotting: Every two to five years in late spring. Be careful not to tear at the roots when you untangle them. If you see a white fluffy substance around the roots, you're in luck! This is a beneficial mycorrhyzal fungus that helps the tree digest nutrients. Root aphids also appear white and fluffy, but they move!

Use a mix of 20 percent organic matter to 80 percent grit, or Akadama with 30 percent grit added.

Pruning: Prune in late summer to early autumn when the wounds are less likely to bleed resin, which stains the bark white. Seal wounds immediately. When removing branches, consider leaving a stub and shaping it into a jin.

Keep the branches in proportion by pruning back the outer twigs to healthy adventitious shoots which appear on older wood. These can then be wire-trained and grown on to replace the outer twigs until they, too, will eventually be pruned back and the process is repeated.

Pinching: Break off the tips of the new shoots as they extend (see page 62 for detailed information on pinching pines), and pull out all old needles in late summer.

Watering: Keep the soil moist but don't saturate it. Pines prefer very free-draining soil so, to be safe, it is best to shelter them from prolonged rainfall.

Feeding: Half-strength solution of balanced food throughout summer and one nitrogen-free feed in autumn, plus a single application of slow-release organic fertilizer in mid-winter.

Beware! Black pines are prone to root rot if the soil remains wet for too long. Ensure that the soil is very free-draining and shelter the tree from prolonged rainfall, especially in winter.

Pistacia terebinthus
Pistachio

Indoor

Pistachios are found in the Mediterranean region as well as in the Far East, where commercial bonsai are produced. They are sub-tropical plants, never growing much bigger than a large shrub.

The thick, glossy-green compound leaves are borne on stiff shoots and appear to grow in all directions, which makes it difficult to keep a small bonsai neat, so it is best to opt for a medium to large bonsai. In spring, when growth is most rapid, the bark thickens dramatically and the branches become brittle as they are pumped full of water. Wiring at this time is a risky business – the branches snap easily and the fleshy bark will separate from the heartwood with the slightest pressure, resulting in the death of the rest of the branch. Unless you are an expert at wiring bonsai, it is better to shape branches by selective pruning – cutting back to a bud which faces in the direction you want the new shoot to grow.

Pistachios are fascinating little trees, with rigid shoots growing in all directions. Once tamed, they make dramatic bonsai and are a good species to experiment on

Where to keep pistachio

Pistachios enjoy full sun when growing in open ground but are less tolerant of it when grown in pots, especially if the sun is intensified through window glass. If your pistachio lives indoors all summer, give it the maximum possible light without allowing it to be exposed to hot afternoon sun. Likewise, if it lives outdoors in summer, it should be positioned where the pot is shaded from the afternoon sun.

Maintenance

Repotting: Every three years or so – more often if the tree appears to be rootbound. The roots are easily crushed, so always use very sharp tools and avoid tearing at the roots when untangling them.

Use standard bonsai soil with some additional organic matter.

Pruning: Pistachios can be pruned at any time of year. The fleshy bark separates easily from the heartwood under pressure, so always use very sharp tools. Wounds heal quite quickly but occasionally die back, especially if the soil is a little on the dry side. Seal wounds immediately to prevent moisture loss and reduce the chance of die-back.

Pinching: The shoots are too tough to pinch with the fingers, so use sharp nail scissors to snip them back to one or two leaves. The compound leaves can appear a little unkempt so, to maintain a neat bonsai, you can try cutting through the central stem of each leaf to leave just two of the leaflets.

This will also help to promote back-budding.

Watering: Keep the soil moist at all times but don't allow it to remain saturated for long periods. Once a week, immerse the pot in a bowl of water for 20 minutes to ensure that there are no dry spots.

Feeding: Balanced food throughout summer and autumn. If temperatures are kept above 68°F (20°C) during winter, the tree might continue growing, although the rate of growth will slow down due to the reduced light levels. If growth does continue during winter, half-strength balanced fertilizer should be applied, but be prepared to stop feeding as soon as growth ceases.

Beware! Pistachios will not tolerate dry roots, so cover the surface of the soil with moss or gravel to reduce evaporation. Standing the pot above a tray of water will increase local humidity and will also help reduce further moisture loss from the leaves.

Podocarpus macrophyllus
Chinese Yew

Indoor

This evergreen conifer is one of the most popular trees in ornamental gardens throughout the Far East, where they are clipped and shaped to resemble miniature versions of full-sized trees – rather like an oversized bonsai growing in the ground. Their popularity is due to the rich, glossy foliage which persists for several years and becomes very dense, not unlike the native yews of Great Britain, to which this species is not related.

In nature, the trunks of *podocarpus* tend to divide into several vertical branches at about a meter above the ground, each branch supporting several horizontal secondary branches bearing flat pads of dense foliage. This habit, if copied, can produce an extremely interesting bonsai. Unfortunately, many commercial growers take leggy seedlings or rooted cuttings and train the stems into all sorts of bizarre shapes – spirals, loops and so on. These gimmicky plants will never make good bonsai and should be left on the shelf.

Where to keep *podocarpus*
Podocarpus enjoy sunshine, so if you can keep yours outdoors in summer you can place it where it will receive full sun all day long, provided you can shade the pot or cover the soil with moss to reduce moisture loss through evaporation. Indoors, the tree should be shaded from hot sun through glass during the hottest part of the day. Create a humid atmosphere by regular spraying and by standing the pot over a tray of water.

Although *podocarpus* are commonly used in Japanese gardens where they are subjected to sub-zero temperatures in winter, they are rather less tolerant of cold when grown in pots. Many growers say that their *podocarpus* have survived zero temperatures without any problem, but others have lost their bonsai at the first hint of frost. To be safe, keep your podocarpus above 41°F (5°C) during winter.

Maintenance
Repotting: Every three years or longer, in late spring. The roots are very sensitive to pruning, so only remove one-eighth of the root mass at any one time. Be very gentle when untangling the roots – the slightest damage will cause the tree to react badly and may result in loss of some shoots and branches. Water sparingly for the first few weeks after repotting to encourage the new roots to extend rapidly in search of water.

Use a standard bonsai soil or Akadama.

Pruning: Branches can be pruned at any time during the growing period. Use very sharp tools at all times and be careful not to crush the bark as you cut. *Podocarpus* are slow to regenerate new growth from old wood, preferring to throw out new shoots from parts of the branches that still bear old foliage.

Pinching: The shoots are too tough and fibrous and the foliage is too dense for finger pinching. Use very sharp nail scissors to cut through the new shoots, allowing just five or six new leaves to remain. Blunt scissors will crush the shoots and cause significant die-back.

Watering: Water regularly in the growing period, reducing water slightly in winter and after repotting. Spray the foliage regularly with fresh water.

Feeding: Half-strength balanced food throughout summer. If the tree is kept warm in winter it will continue growing, albeit at a slower pace, and feeding should continue. Don't feed if the tree stops growing in winter.

Beware! Podocarpus have extremely sensitive roots and react badly to root pruning. If you cut away more than about one-eighth of the roots when repotting, the tree will sulk and may even lose some recent growth. In severe cases the entire tree might collapse. Over watering turns leaves gray.

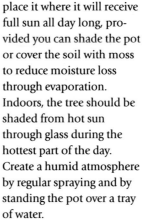

The foliage of this attractive little tree has an unmistakable oriental appearance. Guy wires have been used to hold some stubborn branches in place until they set

Punica granatum
Pomegranate

The Romans were responsible for spreading this attractive small Mediterranean tree throughout the region because of its beautiful bell-shaped red or pink flowers and succulent fruit. Pomegranates are also native to China where most of today's commercial bonsai are grown, although some Mediterranean countries, especially Israel, are taking an increasing share of the market.

Pomegranates are semi-evergreen, which means that they will lose some or all their leaves in winter if temperatures fall below a certain point or if water is scarce. This is not a problem because the three most endearing features of this species are its flowers, fruit, and characterful bark. The bark is smooth buff to brown on young plants, and buds soon develop a stringy texture as the tree matures. The main "veins" directly linking the roots and branches swell at a greater rate than the rest of the bark, and eventually the bark in the spaces between the veins dies. This creates a gnarled and ancient look to the tree which greatly enhances its value.

Where to keep pomegranates
Pomegranates adore the sun and can be exposed to full sun all day long, indoors or out. During the hottest months of the year it is advisable to shade the pots from sun through glass to prevent the roots from "cooking."

If you want your pomegranate to remain evergreen, maintain winter temperatures above 62.6°F (17°C). Below this temperature the tree will lose some or all of its leaves. Never allow the temperature to fall below 41°F (5°C), and protect from cold drafts at all times. Give as much light as possible in winter.

Maintenance
Repotting: Every two or three years in early spring, before growth starts. Old plants can be left for up to five years before repotting.

Use a mix of 50 percent organic matter and 50 percent grit or Akadama mixed with 30 percent grit to ensure good drainage. Use a fairly deep pot.

Pruning: Prune unwanted branches in spring. Hard-prune all branches for structure immediately after flowering and then allow all new shoots to grow unchecked until flower buds can be seen on the shorter, non-extending shoots. At this point you can safely prune back the longer shoots to two or three leaves. These stubs will form the base for next year's flowering shoots.

Opposite: Pomegranates have gnarled bark, twisted trunks, gorgeous flowers and fruit, and yellow autumn leaves. Who could ask for more from a bonsai?

Below right: The bright vermillion, trumpet-shaped flowers are borne in early summer

Pinching: The flowers are borne on short shoots emerging from last year's growth. Restrict pinching to shoots that are over-extending during flowering. Pinching at any other time may restrict flowering.

Watering: Water well at all times. Although pomegranates like free-draining soil they also can be rather thirsty, preferring to grab as much water as possible as it drains through the soil. Water consumption increases while fruit is swelling. In winter reduce watering if the leaves fall.

Feeding: Balanced food until flowering commences, then stop feeding. Resume when flowering has finished, with low-nitrogen fertilizer. If the tree remains in leaf during winter, give a weak dose of slow-release organic balanced food. If your pomegranate is reluctant to flower, apply low-nitrogen fertilizer all summer and for as long into the autumn/ winter as the tree remains in leaf. This should correct the problem within a year.

Beware! The branches on pomegranates are very brittle, even when quite young. Wire-train new shoots while they are still green and pliable, taking care not to create too-sharp angles which will crush the inner tissue and cause the shoot to die.

Pyracantha
Firethorn

Pyracanthas were originally introduced to the West from China and are now one of the most common garden and hedging shrubs throughout the world. In late spring *pyracanthas* explode in a profusion of creamy-white flowers borne in flat pannicles. These usually stand above the branches. In late summer and autumn the weight of the masses of orange or red berries causes them to hang down below the branches. This means that the branches must be well-spaced so that there is plenty of room for both flowers and fruit to be displayed without becoming entangled with the foliage on the next branch.

Many commercial bonsai are sensibly planted on rocks which not only creates a dramatic image, contrasting with the tiny flowers and fruit, but also ensures adequate space below the lowest branches for the autumn fruit to be displayed.

Where to keep *pyracanthas*

All *pyracanthas* prefer to be exposed to full sun. This increases flower and fruit production and keeps growth compact and healthy. In winter hardy *pyracanthas* can survive under a blanket of snow for several weeks, but to be on the safe side it is best to bring them into a garage or shed in really bad weather.

There are an increasing number of tropical *pyracan-*

The spectacular display of early summer flowers is followed by masses of brilliant orange or red berries, which can persist on the tree right through winter

tha bonsai becoming available, mainly from the Philippines. These, too, prefer full sun and are best kept outdoors in summer to maximize pollination so that a good crop of berries is ensured. In winter, however, they must be kept above 44.6°F (7°C).

Maintenance

Repotting: Repot young plants annually and older plants every two years. Use standard bonsai soil.

Pruning: Prune to shape and remove unwanted branches immediately after flowering, taking care not to prune away too many flowering spurs, which would spoil the autumn display of fruit. Allow the new shoots that grow after pruning to extend untouched until the fruit has set, and then cut back to three or four leaves. This shortened shoot will form the base of next year's flowering shoots.

Pinching: Pinch just the over-extending shoots only during flowering and again when fruit is ripe. Pinching at any other time may remove or prevent growth which is necessary for next year's flower production, or encourage more vigorous extension growth.

Watering: Although tolerant of a little dryness around the roots from time to time, firethorn will eventually start to die back if this is allowed to happen too often. Keep the soil evenly moist throughout the year. Be vigilant during winter when *pyracanthas* still consume water.

Feeding: Balanced food until flowering commences, then stop feeding. Resume when flowering has finished, with low-nitrogen fertilizer. If the fruit falls before it has set, try using nitrogen-free food after flowering next year. If your *pyracantha* is reluctant to flower, apply low-nitrogen fertilizer throughout the growing season and change to nitrogen-free in autumn.

Beware! The shoots on *pyracanthas* become brittle in their second year. Wire-train new shoots while they are still green and pliable. The thorns are extremely sharp and can cause painful scratches. These thorns are, in fact, aborted shoots where the apical bud has become modified to form a sharp point. If you snip off the tip of each thorn you will not only make working on the tree a less-painful experience, but you will also encourage the dormant buds at the sides of the thorn to develop.

110

Rhododendron indicum
Satsuki Azalea

Outdoor

In their native Japan, azalea bonsai are in a class of their own. Not only do the smooth orange-brown bark and the small glossy leaves produce wonderful bonsai in their own right, but the profusion of flowers in May and June come in an almost infinite variety of colors. Some varieties have self-colored flowers and some bear flowers of two different colors on the same tree. Others even have pink, white, and variegated flowers. What's more, each year new varieties appear.

The flowers are borne at the tips of the previous year's shoots and, unlike normal garden azaleas,

appear after vegetative growth has appeared from the buds immediately behind the flower bud.

Always buy azalea bonsai when they are in flower, because it is impossible to describe adequately the amazing flower colors on a simple label.

Where to keep azaleas
Satsuki azaleas grow naturally on sheltered mountain slopes or at woodland margins. They will tolerate full sun for a while but will perform at their best if kept in semi-shade, or even full shade during mid-summer. The flowers also last a lot longer in semi-shade.

In winter protect from wind at all times and bring the tree into a frost-free

The variety of color in the flowers of satsuki azaleas is almost infinite. But even without flowers, the sinuous orange/brown trunk and neat glossy foliage make the species ideal for bonsai of all sizes

garage or shed if temperatures threaten to stay below 9°F (-5°C) for more than a day or so.

Maintenance
Repotting: Repot young plants every two years, old plants every four or five years, immediately after flowering. Use only lime-free ingredients, preferably opting for a proprietary ericaceous compost or sphagnum peat for the organic content.

Use standard bonsai mix with an extra 20 percent organic matter. Add a few handfuls of chopped fresh sphagnum moss to keep the soil aerated and to enhance both drainage and water retention.

Pruning: Prune branches and cut back all excess growth immediately after flowering. From then on do

not prune until the same time the following year unless you want to remodel the bonsai.

Pinching: Pinch out the tips of over-extending shoots to keep the tree in trim. Do not automatically pinch out all growing tips in summer or you will find you have thrown away all next year's flowers.

Watering: Azaleas will not tolerate drought so the soil must not be allowed to become even partially dry at any time. Although they love moist soil, azaleas are not particularly thirsty so you will not need to water more often than with any other species. Keep the soil moist but not too wet throughout the year.

IMPORTANT: Azaleas are calcifuges (lime-haters) and will rapidly deteriorate if calcium is allowed to build up in the soil. Use only rain water or lime-free tapwater. If you cannot use either, treat the soil with a proprietary soil acidifier.

Feeding: Weak solution of balanced food until flowering commences, then stop feeding. Resume only when flowering has finished, with low-nitrogen fertilizer until the end of autumn. Ensure that any fertilizers used are suitable for ericaceous plants. Using organic fertilizers at all times will take care of this.

Beware! The shoots and branches are very brittle and tend to snap without warning when being wire trained.

Sageretia theezans Sageretia

Originally from China, sageretia is now used for commercial bonsai production throughout the Far East. It is rightly one of the most popular species of indoor bonsai and is ideal for the first-timer.

The bark is a smooth gray-buff but flakes away in irregular patches to reveal lighter shades beneath, rewarding you with an ever-changing pattern. Branches which are a few years old, and even exposed roots, also adopt this characteristic.

When young the shoots are surprisingly brittle, but they become more supple in time, so any wiring should be done after they have begun to mature. However, although the shoots emerge from the parent branch at a wide angle, sometimes as much as 90 degrees, very little wiring should be necessary. The shoots are so prolific that branches can be grown and shaped merely by selective pruning.

Where to keep sageretias

In nature sageretia lives in the dappled shade of taller trees and quickly becomes droopy and tired if exposed to hot sun. Shade provided by an open-weave net curtain would be ideal if the tree is close to a sunny window. An east or northwest-facing window would probably not need any shade. Sageretias appreciate fresh air so, if possible, keep your bonsai outdoors in summer. Here it should be kept in dappled shade. Bring it indoors at night in early and late summer, when nights can be chilly.

In winter, temperatures must be maintained above 54°F (12°C) to prevent damage. When kept above 63°F (17°C) the tree may continue growing all winter if placed in a bright location.

Maintenance

Repotting: Every two to three years. Use a very sharp tool to cut the tough thicker roots. Use standard bonsai soil or Akadama.

Pruning: The wood of sageretia is very hard and requires sharp tools and a strong grip. Pruning can take place at any time of year but is best done in mid-winter. Thin out crowded areas when growth has stopped or is at its slowest. Thinning while the tree is actively growing will encourage too much new growth. Conversely, if you want to build up the foliage mass on an underdeveloped

Tiny leaves, vigorous growth and colorful, flaky bark make sageretia an ideal species for the novice

branch, prune the branch back in mid-summer and it will respond with masses of vigorous new growth.

Pinching: Shoots are too tough and too numerous to pinch with the fingers effectively. Use sharp scissors to trim the foliage to shape but don't cut through individual leaves or they will discolor and spoil the tree.

Watering: Sageretias are not thirsty and therefore can tolerate dry roots. Water prolifically during the summer and whenever the tree is growing. Ease off the water a little as growth slows or stops in winter. Never spray the foliage.

Feeding: Balanced food while the tree is actively growing. Reduce frequency as growth slows down and stop if growth stops completely. Wait for two weeks after growth recommences before resuming feeding.

Beware! The two worst enemies of sageretia are cold drafts and dry air. Keep local humidity high by standing the pot over a tray of water and protect from drafts at all times. Mildew is a major problem, as is white fly.

Serissa foetida
Tree of a Thousand Stars

Indoor

This romantically named plant really is a most charming subject for bonsai, with tiny glossy leaves, bark that quickly becomes fissured and gnarled, and a willingness to produce masses of minute white trumpet-shaped flowers at any time of year. Although little more than a low, spreading shrub in the wild, it will develop strong vertical trunks with careful bonsai training. Frequently multi-trunked styles or group plantings are produced to maximize the foliage and flower display with relatively immature material.

Because *serissas* are such vigorous growers and so obliging to the bonsai enthusiast, they are one of the most popular species and are ideal for the beginner. It is worth buying several small trees and planting them in larger pots to encourage them to gain bulk rapidly while you practice your bonsai techniques on them.

Where to keep serissas
Serissas are deceptively sturdy little plants and are able to bounce back after various traumas such as cold drafts, a short period of dry soil, and so on. But it would be a mistake to assume that just because your bonsai recovered once, it will do so the next time. To be safe, don't expose your serissa to temperatures below 54°F (12°C) at any time. Even at this temperature some foliage may be lost. Ideally, keep the temperature above 68°F (20°C) all year round.

Serissas will take full sun quite happily, provided the heat does not cause the soil to dry out. Using a deep pot can help.

Maintenance
Repotting: Every two to three years in early spring. It is not for nothing that this species is called "foetida," as the roots and lower trunk emit an obnoxious smell when wet – which they always are. This is unnoticeable on a bonsai in normal conditions, but when you start prodding around and scuffing the bark, this dainty little tree can become quite bad-mannered!

Use standard bonsai soil with an extra 20 percent organic matter.

Pruning: Prune unwanted branches at any time. Thin out overcrowded areas when growth is at its slowest, to avoid inducing excessive adventitious shoots. Pruning in summer will cause masses of vigorous shoots to appear at many points in the vicinity of the cut. The harder you prune, the more shoots will grow.

Pinching: Use nail scissors to trim the foliage clouds to shape. Avoid cutting through leaves, as this will cause them to discolor.

Watering: *Serissas* love a really humid atmosphere. Do not over-water or stand for hours in water. However, you can stand the pot directly in a tray of water for a short while. Spray as often as you can with tepid water.

Feeding: Balanced food while the tree is actively growing. If growth continues in winter, apply weak low-nitrogen fertilizer.

Beware! Although *serissas* like plenty of moisture in the soil and a humid atmosphere, the flowers do not last long if they are allowed to remain damp for too long. Be careful not to wet the flowers when watering, and ensure that there is good air circulation when spraying so the flowers dry quickly.

Serissas are normally trained with bizarrely-shaped trunks, accentuated by the stringy bark. The minute leaves and profusion of white flowers make this species one of the most popular of all indoor bonsai

Stewartia monadelpha Stewartia/ Stuartia

Outdoor

This dwarf variety of the native Japanese species is one of the few bonsai subjects that looks better in winter and early spring than at any other time. The leaves are a little too large in summer, even after regular pinching over a number of years, although the autumn color can be quite spectacular. The broad white flowers are also out of proportion and are therefore not worth actively encouraging.

In winter the gorgeous smooth, orange bark, which even covers the current year's growth, glows like fire against the dark sky, and the upward-pointing buds look like little green candle flames. The beauty, grace, and elegance of this species is almost impossible to describe.

Stewartias have a strong vertical habit which makes broad, spreading styles impractical. Branches that are wired down to the vertical quickly lose vigor and throw out adventitious shoots which rocket upward. It is far better to follow nature when shaping your stewartia than to try to conquer it.

Where to keep stewartias

Stewartias can tolerate hot sun but prefer slightly dappled shade, especially in really hot weather. Drying winds can also cause leaf margins to scorch. The ideal position for your stewartia would be where it receives full sun in the morning but is shaded from mid-day onward by a nearby tree or house so that there is still good overhead light.

In winter your stewartia will withstand several degrees of frost for short periods, but should be placed in a frost-free shed or garage in really cold weather. Try not to expose to temperatures below 9°F (-5°C).

Maintenance

Repotting: Every two to five years in early spring, cutting thick roots back hard. Stewartias are lime-haters, so use only guaranteed lime-free soil ingredients such as ericaceous composts or sphagnum peat. A mix of 80 percent organic matter and 20 percent grit will help retain sufficient moisture. Akadama can be used if you are on hand to water twice a day if necessary.

Pruning: Prune branches in early spring, three weeks before repotting. Hollow out the wounds and immediately seal them to prevent unsightly swelling as they heal. Prune the previous season's shoots back to an outward-facing bud.

Pinching: Pinch out the growing tip of all shoots as soon as two full leaves have been produced. Continue throughout the growing season. Remove any unwanted adventitious or inward-growing shoots as soon as they appear.

Watering: Stewartias are water-lovers as well as lime-haters so if you want to keep one and your tapwater is hard (lime-rich), you will need to collect an awful lot of rainwater! You need to keep the soil as wet as possible without becoming waterlogged all year, reducing the moisture content slightly in winter.

Feeding: Balanced food during summer and nitrogen-free in autumn. Use only ericaceous fertilizers or those recommended for calcifuges (lime-haters) such as heathers, camellias, and so on.

Beware! Stewartias are not the easiest of species to keep healthy, but the extra effort is worthwhile. It will probably take you a couple of seasons to get the maintenance right but you will be well rewarded.

114

Although the flowers and foliage of stewartia are both attractive in their own right, most bonsai connoisseurs prefer the winter image, when the orange bark and flame-shaped buds can be fully appreciated

Ulmus parvifolia
Chinese Elm

Indoor & Outdoor

This is the perfect species for the newcomer to bonsai. It can be grown indoors or out, can withstand sun and cold, has small leaves and produces new shoots from all parts of the tree at the drop of a hat. The leaves are borne alternately at regular short intervals on the shoots and, after pinching, a new shoot appears from the base of almost every leaf. This produces a herring-bone pattern of growth which is so predictable that even the novice can quickly learn to prune and shape with complete confidence.

There are several forms of Chinese elm, some with smooth bark and others which rapidly develop thick, corky bark. The smooth-bark varieties tend to be slightly less hardy and need acclimatizing before they can be exposed to the cold. If you want to keep your Chinese elm outside all year, it is best to look for one with corky bark to avoid the risk of disappointment.

Where to keep Chinese elms

Full sun is fine in early and late summer but some light shade is beneficial in the hottest months. Dappled shade is mandatory if Chinese elms are kept indoors, close to a sunny window. On the other hand, they are perfectly happy in shadier conditions. In fact the leaf condition and autumn color might even improve, although growth will be somewhat coarser.

In winter, Chinese elms are deciduous if kept outdoors and more or less evergreen indoors. Temperatures below 9°F (-5°C) can cause root damage and die-back of fine shoots so provide frost-free conditions in really bad weather. Shelter from winds and prolonged rain in winter.

Chinese elms may suffer foliage loss after a change in position or local environment, but this does not harm the plant and it will soon recover.

Maintenance

Repotting: Every one to three years in early spring. The bark on the roots is slimy and fibrous and is easily damaged under pressure or if blunt tools are used. Always use very sharp tools and cut with a single, positive action. Use standard bonsai soil or Akadama.

Pruning: Prune unwanted branches in early spring, three weeks before or after repotting. Pruning in mid-summer will generate masses of new growth from

Chinese elms rapidly produce a fine, dense tracery of twigs, bearing small, neat leaves. The bark of some varieties also becomes deeply fissured at a fairly young age

around the wound. Weak branches can be strengthened by hard-pruning in mid-summer and allowing the new shoots to develop.

Pinching: Pinch out the tops of all new shoots, leaving one or two leaves on each. Thin out congested areas and dead shoots as it becomes necessary, which will probably be at least twice a year.

Watering: Maintain evenly moist in summer and only slightly drier in winter. Chinese elms can be especially thirsty in spring and early summer.

Feeding: Balanced food while the tree is actively growing. If growth continues in winter, apply weak low-nitrogen fertilizer. Outdoors apply nitrogen-free food in autumn.

Beware! Never use systemic insecticides or fungicides on Chinese elms. For some reason these can cause total defoliation and considerable loss of vigor which can result in some die-back. Fortunately this species is relatively pest-free.

Wisteria
Wisteria

Wisterias are probably the most spectacular of all garden climbers, with their profusion of purple to pink hanging racemes of small pea-like flowers which appear in late spring and early summer. In some years a second flush of flowers appears in early autumn. Growth is extremely rapid; sometimes shoots can extend over a meter a week. Wisteria can live to an immense age – well over a hundred years – and can develop massive swirling trunks, full of hollows and crevices.

Wisteria is also one of the most spectacular bonsai species – when in flower. Unfortunately, for the rest of the time they are scruffy, rampant-growers that are impossible to tame. But don't let that deter you. There is no sight so breathtaking as a specimen wisteria bonsai in full bloom.

A wisteria bonsai consists of little more than an interesting trunk and sparse, stubby branches which form the framework for the year's frantic activity. Branches can normally be developed and improved by selective pruning alone, and wiring only becomes necessary in the early stages of development. In time the trunk and branches will become every bit as characterful as ancient full-sized plants.

Wisterias can make interesting trees even without flowers, but it is the June display of cascading lilac blooms that are the real appeal of this species

Where to keep wisterias

Being climbers, wisterias are designed to have their roots in the cool, moist, humus-rich soil in the shade of taller trees, with their shoots climbing through the canopy until their leaves are exposed to full sun. All you need to do is imitate these conditions in your garden or back yard and your bonsai will be perfectly happy. Shade the pot and spray it liberally with water at every opportunity to keep it cool and moist.

In winter the roots can suffer damage in prolonged freezing conditions, especially when wet, so some protection against the worst weather is advisable.

Wisteria can do quite well if kept in a well-ventilated conservatory or cool greenhouse all year, provided temperatures are allowed to fall regularly to below 50°F (10°C).

Maintenance

Repotting: Every three years or so in early spring. Check annually to see if the roots have become potbound. If so, repot immediately; if not, wait another year. Select a deep pot to help keep the roots cool and moist and to balance visually the pendulous flowers. Use standard bonsai soil with some extra organic matter or Akadama.

Pruning:
Structural pruning such as branch removal or shortening the trunk can be done in early spring. The routine pruning technique used on wisteria is specifically designed to encourage flowers. Cut back hard immediately after flowering, removing about half the flower-bearing stubs.

Allow all subsequent growth total freedom until the rapidly extending shoots begin to become a nuisance, and then cut back to two or three buds. This process may be repeated several times each year.

Pinching: Don't pinch.

Watering: Water as lavishly as you like during summer. Deep pots can even be stood in water without the risk of "drowning" the tree. Shallow pots will need watering several times a day in hot weather, so should be avoided.

Feeding: Low-nitrogen food liberally applied from the end of flowering until early autumn; then switch to nitrogen-free food.

Beware! Hot, dry roots quickly shrivel and die, sometimes killing one side of the tree.

Zelkova serrata
Zelkova/Gray Bark Elm

Although closely related to elms, zelkovas are in fact a distinct species. Their natural habit is that of the archetypal tree: a straight, cylindrical trunk which is clear of branches for about two meters, at which point it divides into a number of branches which fan out and fork uniformly in all directions. At the periphery the twigs become very fine and bear neat pointed oval leaves.

Zelkova bonsai follow the same pattern in miniature and are created by shortening the trunk of a young

sapling in mid-summer and training the shoots that emerge from the wound into branches. Very little wiring is necessary because the growth is uniform and generally well-distributed, allowing the fan-like branch structure to be developed by pruning alone.

The bark remains smooth and relatively featureless throughout the tree's life, but this is in total harmony with the elegant and gentle tapering of the branches into the tracery of fine twigs. A gnarled or fissured bark would look incongruous on such a tree.

In the wild, zelkovas naturally form a large, dome-shaped tree. This habit is echoed in bonsai, and a convincing little tree like this can be achieved in just a few years

Some nurseries offer a plant called *"Zelkova sinica,"* but these are generally a variety of Chinese elm *(Ulmus parviflora)* which has been renamed – probably to avoid import restrictions.

Where to keep zelkovas

Zelkovas are perfectly happy in full sun, although in really hot weather the leaves may scorch or become yellowish and leathery and little use to the plant. Regular spraying can help prevent this, but it is more practical to put the tree in semi-shade for the summer, returning it to the sun in late summer or early autumn to enhance the autumn coloration. If kept in semi-shade all year the leaves will retain their spring color – a bronze tint often edged with deep red – well into summer.

In winter the roots will withstand considerable periods of freezing but the delicate fine twigs may die back, especially if exposed to wind for just a short time. Winter protection from the wind is mandatory.

Maintenance

Repotting: Every one to three years, depending on the size and age of the tree, in early spring. Pay attention to the formation of the root buttress at the base of the trunk and prune away crossing or unsightly roots. Use standard bonsai soil or Akadama.

Pruning: Prune unwanted branches in early spring, two weeks before repotting. Strengthen weak branches by pruning them hard in

mid-summer and allowing the resulting new shoots to develop freely until autumn.

Pinching: Pinch out the tops of all new shoots as soon as two leaves have formed. This may well become a weekly task in summer.

Watering: Keep the soil evenly moist throughout the year. Spray the foliage at each watering to keep it fresh, and spray the trunk to keep it free of algae.

Feeding: Balanced food from spring to late summer, then change to nitrogen-free until the leaves have turned color.

Beware! Zelkovas can become congested, especially at the top, which can result in die-back of many fine twigs. Regular thinning of crowded areas is essential.

Appendix

How can you take a summer vacation when your bonsai need daily watering at that time of year? How on earth can they survive sub-zero temperatures in winter? What tools will you need to buy? Here are some answers...

While You Are Away

Providing the daily attention a bonsai requires is easy enough for most of the year. But you will inevitably want to take a vacation at some point. True bonsai devotees will either not take vacations at all or will arrange them during the winter months, when their trees demand less-frequent attention and can generally be left unattended for a couple of weeks. But most of us prefer to take our vacations in the summer. So what measures can we take to ensure our precious trees are still alive and healthy when we return?

Care services
Most reputable specialty bonsai nurseries will offer a vacation-care service for a small fee – or even free – provided your collection isn't too extensive. You have the reassurance of knowing that your bonsai are being cared for by people who have the knowledge and skill to do the job properly, and who may be able to notice any problems that you may have overlooked, such as difficult-to-spot pests or diseases.

Good neighbors
Friends and neighbors are usually willing to water your trees for you for short periods. In fact, many would be quite honored at being asked. But remember that, unless they too are bonsai enthusiasts, they will need thorough training before being allowed to take full responsibility for your collection. Invite them over on a couple of occasions to watch you perform routine watering. Explain the importance of a thorough watering and point out which trees require more than others. Overwatering is not likely to be a problem for two weeks in summer, whereas drought certainly will!

Capillary watering
If you can't find someone to help you out, you can try this technique, using capillary matting – the kind used in greenhouses and available from most garden nurseries. Cut a piece to fit snugly inside the base of the pot and some long strips which are passed up through the drainage holes. (Be careful when easing the tree from the pot and replacing it after positioning the matting.) Stand the pot on stones to raise the strips of matting clear of the bench and immerse the free ends of the strips in a reservoir of water. The strips act as wicks and draw water through the drainage holes and saturate the

It only takes a few minutes to erect a makeshift winter shelter using some old building blocks and a sheet of clear polythene

matting inside the pot. Although this method does not ensure even distribution of water throughout the pot, it will at least keep the tree alive for as long as the reservoir lasts. It is a good idea to place both tree and reservoir in the shade.

Last resort
If all else fails, and you are unable to find help or a supply of capillary matting, there is still one thing you can do. Find the shadiest corner of the garden and bury the pots in the ground, ensuring that the surface of the soil in the pots is below ground level. Scatter some slug pellets around the area, but not too close to the

trunks as this will only encourage the slugs and snails to come too close for comfort. Finally, water the surrounding area well and erect a temporary polythene tent over the trees to conserve as much water as possible. In theory this method should keep the trees well for several weeks – the only danger being if the sun is allowed to fall on the polythene tent and causes the surface of the ground to dry out.

Outdoor Bonsai in Winter

Although most temperate species that are used for bonsai are hardy – i.e., able to withstand freezing – when grown in containers they don't have the advantage of having their roots buried deep in the ground where they are insulated to a certain extent from the cold. They also have fewer buds and finer twigs and shoots which the cold can penetrate more easily.

Most hardy species will tolerate frozen roots for a short time, some for quite long periods, provided that there is no demand placed on them. If the day-time temperature increases so that the buds begin to swell, or the wind causes dehydration of fine shoots or evergreen needles, frozen roots will not be able to replace the lost moisture. Having said that, many hardy species, particularly conifers, actually need a period of sub-zero temperatures in order to remain healthy and build up vigor for the spring growth surge.

The secret of success is to allow the trees to undergo the natural dormancy process but to protect them from the most dangerous of the elements: wind and, to some extent, excessive rain.

Many hardy deciduous species will take overnight frost without any trouble at all, and provide you with the bonus of a beautifully emphasized tracery of fine shoots

If you can provide a "polytunnel" (polythene greenhouse) for your trees during winter, your problems will largely be solved. This will allow light and air to reach the trees but will shelter them from both wind and rain. If this is not possible, you can cover the display benches with clear polythene and place the trees underneath, standing the pots on bricks to keep them off the ground.

Whether your trees are in a polytunnel or in makeshift winter quarters, you will need to check them each week to make sure the pots are not drying out. In mild weather open the tunnel or tent for a few hours to allow a change of air.

If neither of these provisions are possible, there is still one course of action you can take. Conifers can be placed against a fence or wall where they are sheltered from north and east winds. Cover the surface of the pots with plastic bags to keep off the worst of the rain. Large deciduous bonsai (except trident maples and Chinese elms) can receive similar treatment. Smaller ones, and Chinese elms and trident maples of all sizes, should be eased from their pots and planted in the ground in a sheltered corner of the garden.

Ensure the top of the root ball is at least an inch or so beneath ground level. It is a good idea to buy some horticultural fleece (a fibrous sheeting – extremely lightweight and with excellent insulating properties) to drape over the tops of the trees. This will allow passage of rain but greatly reduces the wind and maintains a temperature beneath which is constantly several degrees higher than outside.

The only danger with the latter type of winter provision is that soil-borne pests may attack the roots. This will not normally happen in the depth of winter, but as spring approaches and the soil warms up, pests become active. You would be wise not to leave it too late before lifting your trees from the ground and replacing them in their pots.

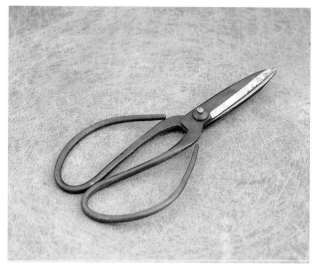

Tools

The serious bonsai enthusiast will gradually build up a wide variety of specialty tools, including several kinds of pruning cutters, shears, pliers; wire cutters, scrapers, and so on. However, to begin with you can do just as well with normal household or garden tools. You will need cutters, small scissors, pliers, and wire cutters and, provided they are all sharp, they will serve you well.

However, as you become more involved in your hobby, you will probably begin to build up your own collection of specialty tools. This selection will give you an idea of the most common Japanese bonsai tools and their uses.

Above: Angled side cutters for pruning branches

Top right: Strong shears for pruning roots

Center: Coconut-fiber brush for tidying the soil

Right: Wire cutters that cut right to the tip

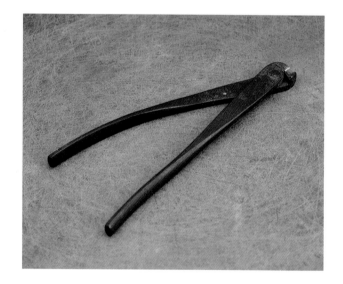

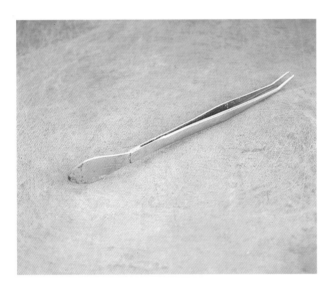

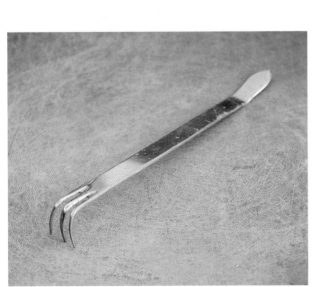

Above: Fine-pointed scissors for pruning shoots

Left: Tweezers to make tip-pinching easier

Below: Small root rake, good for weeding pots

Glossary

This glossary includes botanical and arboricultural terms which are relevant to bonsai culture as well as terms which are unique to bonsai.

Acid Term describing soils with a pH content of less than 7.0. Although most trees will grow happily in acid soil, some. including field maple (*Acer campestre*) and beech (*Fagus sylvatica*) do better in more alkaline conditions. Others, particularly azaleas, rhododendrons, and some heathers, will thrive only in acid soils.

Acuminate Tapering to a fine point, usually referring to leaf shapes.

Alkaline A term describing soils with a pH content of more than 7.0, or calcium-rich. Although many trees will grow happily in alkaline soil, others prefer more acid conditions. Some species, including azaleas, rhododendrons, and some heathers will not tolerate alkaline soil at all. These plants are known as calcifuges.

Alternate Describing leaves or buds which are placed singly at different levels on alternate sides of a shoot.

Apex The tip of a shoot or root, or of a tree, from which extension growth takes place. In bonsai this point is decided upon for aesthetic reasons and is therefore not necessarily the focus of the plant's energy.

Axil, axillary The angle between a leaf and the stem from which future growth can emerge. The angle between the midrib and the vein of a leaf.

Bankan Bonsai style: a tree with a twisted or coiled trunk.

Basal Applied to fresh growth arising from the base of a plant.

Bonkei A "potted landscape"

consisting of rocks, small trees, and other plants, and always with miniature figures, houses or bridges.

Bonsai Literally a "potted plant," the term has now come to mean the (traditionally Chinese and Japanese) art of creating in miniature the splendor of a fully grown tree by careful and meticulous pruning and shaping of a tree growing in a (usually shallow) container.

Break To grow out from an axillary bud. This growth pattern is often natural but in bonsai it is normally the result of pruning or pinching current shoots, and forms the basis of most refinement techniques as well as the Lignan or "grow-and-clip" method of development.

Broad-leaved Denotes any tree other than conifer.

Broom Bonsai style generally based on the natural growth habit of zelkova, where all the branches arise from the same point, at the top of a straight trunk. All branches are more or less equal in weight and subdivide at diminishing intervals, forming a regular dome-shaped crown. Japanese term: Hokidachi.

Bud notching Cutting a small crescent of bark from above a bud to stimulate growth from that bud and to encourage a wide angle between the resulting shoot and the main branch. A useful if somewhat under-employed technique in bonsai.

Bunjingi Bonsai style: the only named style to originate in China and based on the representations of trees in the paintings of the southern school of landscape painting which began back in the Tang dynasty (618-906). The name derives from the scholars who were known as Wen-jen or "men of books."

Buttress The exaggerated thickening of the trunk base at the point where the surface roots emerge. This highly desirable feature gives a tree a feeling of stability and strength.

Calcifuge Plant which cannot tolerate the presence of lime in the soil, or a pH of more than 7.0. Rhododendrons, azaleas, and heathers are among these.

Channeled Describing a leaf whose margins curl upward, forming a channel.

Chokkan Bonsai style: a tree with a straight upright trunk known as "formal upright." The ideal chokkan bonsai will have a perfectly straight trunk with uniform taper and branch structure and an overall conical shape. The roots should be spread evenly around the base.

Classification The internationally recognized system of classifying plants. Latin names are used since many plants do not have common names, and most common names vary considerably between countries and even between regions within one country.

Clone Identical plants arising from a single parent and reproduced vegetatively. All lombardy poplars (*Populus nigra "Italica"*) are male clones and are therefore all offspring of one original male parent.

Columnar Describes a tree which is tall and narrow with straight, more or less parallel sides.

Conifer A cone-bearing tree, usually with needle-like or linear leaves.

Container-grown Young nursery stock which has been raised in pots of one form or another.

Coppicing The practice of cutting trees back to their base in order to encourage the growth of several new stems. Almost invariably carried out on deciduous species. The word "copse" is a corruption of "coppice."

Cutting A section of stem leaf or root which is taken in order to propagate the plant and maintain identical characteristics.

Damping off A disease which may be caused by several different fungi that attacks young seedlings, causing the stems to collapse at ground level and killing the plant. It is encouraged by cold wet soils, overcrowding, or poor air circulation around the stem. Damping off may be prevented by watering the compost with Cheshunt compound when sowing, and again once the seedlings have germinated. Other precautions include avoiding reusing old composts, and thoroughly cleaning all seed trays and tools before use.

Deciduous Describes a tree or shrub which loses its leaves at the end of each growing season.

Deltoid Describes a leaf which is triangular-shaped or with curved basal angles; for example, the leaf of the silver birch.

Derris An insecticide obtained from the root of a tropical climbing plant. Although it is not as effective as modern synthetic insecticides, it is kinder to the plant and less persistent.

Die-back When shoots, twigs, and sometimes whole branches wither and dry out. Major causes include drought (birches, willow), late spring frosts (Japanese maples, Chinese elm, etc.), and severe winter weather (most imported plants). Root damage or disease can also cause die-back. All dead or dying wood should be removed without delay to prevent the spread of any resulting infection to live tissue.

Disbudding Removing unwanted buds in order to direct the plant's energy into the remaining ones. This may be done to increase the size and quality of blooms, but in bonsai it is more often used as a shaping technique, especially with shohin

(small-size) bonsai.

Division Propagation by separating sections from the root mass of a plant. These sections must have buds or shoots as well as adequate roots. Most trees and shrubs which either naturally grow in clumps, such as hazel, or which sucker profusely, such as elm, can be propagated this way.

Drainage Probably the most important factor in bonsai composts, drainage is the free passage of water downward through the compost and its dispersal through the drainage holes in the base of the pot. Poor drainage will cause waterlogged soil, which in turn will provide ideal conditions for root-rotting fungi. It will also prevent sufficient air space, thus further weakening the roots.

Driftwood A bonsai style – Sharimiki – comprising large areas of bare, bleached wood, often carved and shaped into detailed abstract designs. This style above all others creates the impression of immense age and durability. Unlike other bonsai styles, these do not have to be particularly treelike to be successful. It is possible to let aesthetic or emotional considerations outweigh traditional bonsai concepts.

Dwarf A genetic mutation of a species, producing a much lower, slower, and more compact growth pattern. Some dwarf species make good bonsai, and their use should only be considered cheating if their natural habit is relied upon too heavily at the expense of more precise bonsai training techniques.

Fastigiate Describes a tall, narrow, columnar growth habit, usually of trees and shrubs, where all the branches sweep sharply upwards.

Feathering A process by which young saplings are allowed to retain their lower branches for a few years in order to thicken and strengthen the trunk.

Fire-blight A severe and almost inevitably fatal fungal disease of trees, particularly those of the family Rosaceae (cherries, apples, cotoneaster, pyracantha, etc.).

Forcing Accelerating the growth cycle of a plant by artificially changing its growing conditions. The most common application of this technique in bonsai cultivation is to encourage late spring-flowering trees to bloom early in time for exhibitions.

Fukinagashi The windswept style of bonsai. Although this is one of the most dramatic of all bonsai styles, it is one of the most difficult to achieve convincingly. Consequently, really fine fukinagashi bonsai are rare and highly prized.

Genus A group of closely related species. For example, all the cherries, apricots, and plums belong to the genus Prunus. The plural is Genera.

Go-kan A bonsai style with five trunks. The individual trunks may be upright, slanted, or curved, but as long as there are five of them the name still applies.

Grafting The bonding of one part of a woody plant to another, usually on a separate plant. There are many different methods of grafting; most involve uniting a plant of desirable characteristics onto the roots of a closely related but sturdier species.

Han-kengai The bonsai style known as semicascade. This, as the name implies, is one of those "in-between" styles whose exact definition is elusive. The most commonly accepted definition is a tree whose leader or most dominant low branch (which must be greater than the ascending leader) cascades below the rim of the pot but not below the base. Much would seem to depend on the depth of the pot, which may be changed from time to time, thus changing the style of the tree almost arbitrarily.

Half-hardy see Hardy.

Hardening-off The process of gradually introducing a plant which has been grown in sheltered or protected conditions to the rigors of the outside environment. This is done by allowing it to stay outside in the open during the day, or in mild spells, and returning the plant to its protection at night.

Hardy Describes a plant which is able to survive outside during the winter.

Hokidachi The bonsai style known as broom or besom. This is probably the most "tree-like" of all bonsai styles and consists of a number of branches all issuing from the same point at the top of an upright trunk. These branches divide and sub-divide regularly until they form a fine tracery of twigs.

Hybrid The offspring of parents of different species, or different forms of a species.

Ikadabuki Raft-style bonsai. This style is created by laying a tree on its side and training all the conveniently placed branches upwards. All the branches which point downward or which are not suitably sited are removed. The original trunk is then buried in the soil and eventually produces roots along its length. The new trunks are then trained in the normal way into any suitable style. Eventually it will be possible to remove all the original root ball, allowing the tree to be supported by the new roots. This is an ideal method for producing group plantings, since there is no competition between individual plants.

Inflorescence The flower-bearing part of a plant.

Internode The distance between the leaf nodes on a shoot. It is this distance which dictates whether or not a particular plant has the growth characteristics suitable for bonsai culture.

Jin The most commonly used Japanese term in bonsai culture, and one of the most difficult to define concisely. A jin is a branch or the apex of a tree which has had its bark removed and has been treated with a preservation bleach such as lime sulphur in order to simulate the naturally occurring dead sun-bleached branches commonly found on old pines and junipers. The judicious use of jins can have a great effect on the aesthetics of a bonsai by counterbalancing areas of foliage where another area of foliage would be considered too heavy. A terminal or apical jin can also be used to create the illusion of a fine tip to a tree where this effect would, for one reason or another, be impossible to achieve with foliage. The appearance of great age and a lifetime's struggle against the elements can be bestowed on a bonsai by the use of jins, which may also be carved and shaped into abstract sculptural forms.

Jukei The Japanese word for "style," describing the shape or form of a bonsai.

Kabudachi Clump-style bonsai, where all the trunks emanate from closely located points on the same root. This style is often created by cutting a trunk down to ground level and allowing several new trunks to grow from around the cut. In full-sized trees this process is known as coppicing.

Kengai Cascade-style bonsai. To qualify as a true cascade the lowest point of the tree must be below the bottom of its container.

Korabuki Multi-trunked style of bonsai.

Kyuhon-yose A nine-trunked bonsai.

Kyonal A proprietary Japanese product used for dressing wounds after pruning. It has a clay-like consistency but never dries out or goes hard. This means that as the wound heals the kyonal is forced out and does not become enveloped by the new growth. It is easy to use, and colored so as to conceal the wound and blend with the bark.

Layering A means of propagation from woody shoots or branches involving the removal of a band of bark around the chosen shoot about one and one-half times the thickness of the shoot. The shoot is then either pegged to the ground and covered with soil or wrapped with damp sphagnum moss and enclosed in polythene. After a time roots should appear, and once they have established the shoot can be severed from the parent and potted.

Leaching The process by which nutrients and other soluble minerals are removed from the soil by water draining through. To counteract this phenomenon, bonsai growers recommend applying more regular (but weaker) feeds.

Leader The main, vertical stem or shoot of a young plant. The dominant shoot which extends fastest and dictates the directional thrust of the tree's growth. Also used to describe the dominant shoot on a branch or smaller twig.

Leaf mold Partially decayed dead leaves which have broken down to a crumbly texture and which should be used as a substitute for peat. Deciduous leaves, especially oak and beech, are suitable for deciduous trees, whereas pine needle mold is best for pines. A mixture of the two when used instead of peat will benefit the trees and is less environmentally destructive.

Loam A soil which is neither heavy and sticky nor dry and sandy. A good loam contains a proportion of clay, sand, humus, and silt, and is both moisture-retentive and free-draining.

Maiden A newly grafted tree, usu-ally only a year or so old, still in the early stages of training. Normally applied to fruit trees.

Mame bonsai Miniature bonsai. Sources vary in the actual definition of the size of mame: some books of Japanese origin state 4 in. high, others 6 in. high. The consensus seems to be, however, that a mame bonsai is one which can easily be held on the flat palm of a hand. In Japan good mame bonsai are almost as perfect in detail as larger trees, but in the West the specialized skills are only partially developed.

Matsu Japanese for pine.

Moyogi The informal upright style of bonsai. This is the most commonly grown style and has come to encompass many of those trees which do not fall comfortably into another style. The traditional Moyogi has a trunk which gently bends first one way, then the other, in ever diminishing curves, throwing out a branch on each outer curve convexity. In spite of the variety of shapes which are accepted (in the West at least) as Moyogi, the true classical form is as difficult to achieve as any of the other more rigidly defined styles.

Native A plant which is believed to have arrived in this country without the influence of mankind.

Neagari The exposed-root style of bonsai. Ironically, this style is more commonly found in Penjing - the original Chinese form of bonsai - than it is in Japanese trees. The calligraphic and emotive quality of line offered by the exposed roots contrasts sharply with the more solid, mass-oriented styles popular in Japan. Although it is relatively easy to find trees with suitable root systems for this style, it takes many years for the epidermis of the root to harden off and adopt the characteristics of the bark on the rest of the tree. Until this has happened the bonsai will not be successful.

Nebari The visible surface roots of a bonsai. Ideally these should radiate evenly but not uniformly all around the base of the trunk. They should emerge gradually from the trunk and should enter the soil in a natural manner. Nebari which all share the same girth and shape are just as incongruous as one-sided or crossing root systems.

Netsuranari Root-connected style – several trees which all grow from the same root. The trees themselves may be individually trained in any style which suits the species and multi-trunk planting. Naturally occurring netsuranari are root suckers – as in elm or some species of prunus.

Nitrogen One of the three major chemical elements necessary for plant growth. Nitrogen is responsible for healthy leaf and shoot growth, but too much may result in over-vigorous, sappy growth. Nitrogen deficiency results in weak growth and small, yellowish leaves.

pH The pH scale is a means of quantifying the acid/alkaline balance of a soil or compost. The neutral point which suits most plants is around 7.0. A lower figure indicates increased acidity and a higher figure indicates increased alkalinity. Although some plants prefer acid conditions and others prefer alkaline, their range is limited to between 4.5- 9. Anything beyond these extremes is inhospitable to normal plant life. The addition of lime to the soil can increase its pH balance, while it may be decreased by using proprietary brand products such as "Miracid."

Phosphates One of the three major plant nutrients, phosphates are responsible for healthy and vigorous roots and also assist in protecting the plant against diseases. Chemical symbol: P.

Pinching Removing the growing tips of the shoots while still soft using the fingernails or, in the case of most conifers, by gently rolling the tip between finger and thumb.

Pollarding The ancient practice of cutting back all branches to the trunk every few years in order to put the long growths, which regenerate after pollarding, to a variety of uses. Traditionally carried out on willow and ash, pollarded oaks, wychelms, and hornbeams are also quite common. The familiar "mop-headed" willows lining river banks are an unmistakable feature of the rural landscape throughout Europe and beyond.

Propagation The increase of plants either by seed, cutting, layering, division, grafting, or, nowadays, tissue culture.

Pruning The controlled cutting-back of woody parts of a plant, either to promote new growth, influence the flowering pattern, or to aid in the shaping. It is possible to style bonsai using pruning as the only shaping technique, as demonstrated by the Chinese "Lignan" school, sometimes referred to as the clip-and-grow style. The drawback is that your choice of design is limited by the natural growth pattern of the tree. However, it is not possible to style a bonsai without pruning, so this should be one of the first techniques learned by the novice.

Respiration The "breathing" action of a plant. The process involves the exchange of oxygen from the atmosphere with carbon dioxide which is released during the conversion of stored foods into plant energy. In effect the reverse of photosynthesis.

Sabamiki (see sharimiki)
Sankan Triple-trunk bonsai style. The attitudes of the tree may be upright, slanting. windswept, or any other suitable design.

Sapwood The living wood forming the outer layers of the trunk or thick branch of a tree. The sapwood consists of several annual rings and is the means through which water and water-born nutrients are conducted up the tree. Once the sapwood has outlived its usefulness it, in effect, dies and hardens to form the structural heartwood which gives the tree its strength.

Sekijoju Root-over-rock style bonsai.

Shakan Slanting style bonsai

Sharimiki A portion of the trunk of a bonsai which has had the bark removed and the exposed wood has been textured and bleached to emulate weather-torn trees in exposed mountain sites.

Sokan Double- or twin-trunk style of bonsai.

Spur A short lateral side growth which only produces a very short extension each year and usually bears the flower buds.

Sucker A shoot arising from the roots or the underground part of a trunk. Suckers often form a tree's major means of propagation, as with elms, and are always the most easy-to-root cutting material.

Tap root The main downward growing root of a plant or young tree. These roots seldom go down more than five or six feet. Young seedlings and nursery stock will have tap roots which should be cut as high up as possible without removing too many side roots before training begins.

Tender Describes any plant which cannot tolerate frost and is liable to damage or death. All trees sold as indoor bonsai should be treated as tender unless you are familiar with the species and are confident that it can survive low temperatures. Even so, no plant should be introduced to severe cold without a period of acclimatization or hardening off.

Terminal Refers to the upper shoot, flower, or bud. This can be either on the leader (main upward growing branch) or on a lateral or sideways growing branch.

Truncate Describes a leaf whose base, adjacent to the petiole, is flat, giving the appearance of its having been cut.

Variegated Applies to leaves which are patterned with patches of a contrasting color, occasionally pink, more often shades of cream or yellow. The unpredictable nature of this patterning and the general busy-ness of its effect make variegated plants unsuitable for bonsai.

Variety A variation on the species, either naturally occurring or artificially induced. Usually the variety differs in one respect, such as leaf shape or color.

Vegetative Propagation by means other than seed. For example: cuttings, layering, division, or grafting. Some plants naturally take advantage of vegetative propagation and even adopt it as their main means of reproduction. Elms produce suckers, crack willow sheds branches which root, and many tropical species send down aerial roots which become established and form new trees.

Whorl An arrangement of leaves or needles radiating from the same point as in the non-extension growth of larch and cedar.

Yamadori Japanese bonsai term for a collected tree.

Yose-ue Group or multi-trunk style of bonsai.

Index

Page numbers in *italic* refer to the illustrations

A

Acer buergerianum (trident maple), 25, 29, 72, *72*
 A. palmatum (Japanese maple), 19, 29, 36, 43, 52-4, 73, *73*
 A. palmatum "Deshojo/Chishio" (Japanese red maples), 40, 75, *75*
 A. palmatum "Kiyohime," 74, *74*
acid soils, 41
adventitious buds, 37, *64*
air, 43, 46
Akadama soil, 46, *46*
algae, 43
aluminum wire, 66
American buttonwood, 17
anchorage, roots, 32
annealed copper wire, 66, 67
apple, crab (*Malus*), 28, 57, 98, *98*
artificial lighting, 27
Artistic Bonsai Concours, 15
Arundinaria (bamboo), 26, 76, 77
Australia, 17
automatic watering, 43
autumn color, 37
azalea, 15, 29, *33*, 36, 40, 43, 54, 62
 Satsuki (*Rhododendron indicum*), 62, 111, *111*

B

bacterial diseases, 43, 46
bamboo (*Arundinaria*), 26, 76, 77
bamboo, sacred (*Nandina domestica*), 27, 101, *101*
"bar branches," 25
bark, 35
 buying bonsai, 24
 composted bark, 46, 47
 deadwood, 68, 69
beech, 29
 Japanese (*Fagus crenata*), 89, *89*
bitumen-based sealants, 60
bleaching deadwood, 68
blood, dried, 55
bonemeal, 55, 56
"bonsai soils," 46
boron, 55
Bougainvillaea, 26, 78, *78*
branches, 34-5
 extending, 61, *61*
 jins, 67, 68, *68*
 pruning, 60-1, *60*
 shape, 25
 wiring, *65*, 66-7
 xylem, 34-5
bright sunny rooms, 26
Buddhism, 14
buds, 36-7, *37*
 adventitious, 37, *64*
 flower, 62
buttonwood, American, 17
buying bonsai, 22-5

C

calcifuges, 41
calcined clay, 47, *47*
California, 17
cambium, 34, 35, *35*, 37
camellias, 15

"candles," pines, 62-4
capillary action, 33
carbon dioxide, 36
Carmona, 27
 C. microphylla (Fukien tea), 79, *79*
Carpinus (hornbeam), 29, 43, 56, 80, *80*
cascade pots, 52, *55*
cats, 43
cedar, Japanese (*Cryptomeria japonica*), 86, 87
Celtis, 28
 C. sinensis (Chinese hackberry), 81, *81*
Chaenomeles (flowering quince), 28, 82, *82*
Chamaecyparis, 29
 C. obtusa (hinoki cypress), 83, *83*
China:
 history of bonsai, 12, 15, 16
 indoor bonsai, 17-18
Chinese elm (*Ulmus parvifolia*), 26, 115, *115*
Chinese hackberry (*Celtis sinensis*), 81, *81*
Chinese juniper (*Juniperus chinensis*), 28, *28*, 93, *93*
Chinese privet (*Ligustrum sinensis*), 97, *97*
Chinese yew (*Podocarpus microphyllus*), 107, *107*
chlorine, in tapwater, 41
chlorophyll, 36, 37, 55
choosing bonsai, 26-9
choosing pots, 52-4, *52-5*
clay, calcined, 47, *47*
color:
 autumn color, 37
 and light, 40, *41*
 pots, 52-4
"combing" roots, 48, *49*
compost, garden, 47, 55
conifers, *34*
 branches, 25
 deadwood, 67
 leaves, 36
 pruning, 61
 repotting, 49
 wiring, 66
copper wire, 66, 67
Cotoneaster, 28, 57
 C. horizontalis, *84*, 85
crab apple (*Malus*), 28, 57, 98, *98*
crape myrtle (*Lagerstroemia*), 26, 96, *96*
Cryptomeria, 28
 C. japonica (Japanese cedar), 86, 87
cutpaste, 60, 69
Cycas (cycads), 27, 88, *88*
cypress, hinoki (*Chamaecyparis obtusa*), 83, *83*

D

day length, 40
dead branches, buying bonsai, 23
deadwood, 67-9, *67*
deciduous trees, *34*
 branches, 25
 pinching out new growth, 61, *63*
 pruning, 61
 repotting, 49
 wiring, 66
department stores, 22
die-back, 60
dormancy, 37
drafts, 43
drainage, 46, *50*, 51
drainage mesh, 50, *50*
driftwood-style, *19*

dull rooms, 27

E

east-facing rooms, 27
Edo period, 15
elms, 54
 Chinese (*Ulmus parvifolia*), 115, *115*
 gray bark (*Zelkova serrata*), *14*, 117, *117*
embryonic buds, 36

F

Fagus crenata (Japanese beech), 89, *89*
fertilizers, 33, 55-7
 foliar feeds, 42, 56
Ficus (fig), 27, 90, *90*
fig (*Ficus*), 27, 90, *90*
firethorn (*Pyracantha*), 28, 57, 110, *110*
flint, crushed, 47
flowering bonsai:
 choosing pots, 54
 pinching out new growth, 62
flowering quince (*Chaenomeles*), 28, 82, *82*
fluorescent lighting, 27
foliage *see* leaves
foliar feeds, 42, 56
Fukien tea (*Carmona microphylla*), 79, *79*
fungal diseases, 23, 41, 43
fungicides, 68

G

Ginkgo biloba, 29, 91, *91*
grafts, 24, *24*
granite, crushed, 47
gray bark elm (*Zelkova serrata*), *14*, 117, *117*
grit, 46, 47, 51
group plantings, shape, 24

H

hackberry, Chinese (*Celtis sinensis*), 81, *81*
Han dynasty, 12
heartwood, 34, 35
 jins and sharis, 68, 69
hinoki cypress (*Chamaecyparis obtusa*), 83, *83*
history, 12-17
holly, Japanese (*Ilex crenata*), 28, 92, *92*
hornbeam (*Carpinus*), 29, 43, 56, 80, *80*
houseplant fertilizers, 56

I

Ilex crenata (Japanese holly), 28, 92, *92*
immersion watering, 42-3, *42*
indoor bonsai, 17-18
inorganic fertilizers, 55-6
insects, 43
internodes, 40, 61
iron wire, 67
Israel, 18
Italy, 18

J

Japan:
 history of bonsai, 14-15
 outdoor bonsai, 19
Japanese beech (*Fagus crenata*), 89, *89*
Japanese black pine (*Pinus thunbergii*), 15, 24, 28, 105, *105*
Japanese cedar (*Cryptomeria*

japonica), 86, 87
Japanese holly (*Ilex crenata*), 28, 92, *92*
Japanese maple (*Acer palmatum*), 19, 29, 36, 43, 52-4, 73, *73*
Japanese red maples (*Acer palmatum* "Deshojo/Chishio"), 40, 75, *75*
jasmine orange (*Murraya paniculata*), 99, *99*
jins, 25, 67, 68, *68*
Juniperus (junipers), 40, 54, 61-2, *62*, 67, 69
 J. chinensis (Chinese juniper), 28, *28*, 93, *93*
 J. rigida (needle juniper), 28, 94, 95
juvenile foliage, 61, *62*

K

Kenko, Yoshida, 14
Kiyohime maple (*Acer palmatum* "Kiyohime"), 74, *74*
Kokufuten exhibitions, 15
Korea, 18

L

Lagerstroemia (crape myrtle), 26, 96, *96*
leaf mold, 46, 47
leaves, 36-7, *37*
 autumn color, 37
 buds, 36-7, *37*
 buying bonsai, 23
 color, 40, *41*
 drafts, 43
 foliar feeds, 42, 56
 juvenile foliage, 61, *62*
 photosynthesis, 40
 pinching out new growth, 61, *62*
 scorching, 40, *40*
 types, 36
 watering, 42
 wind damage, 43
leggy growth, 40, *40*, 61
lifespan, 35
light, 36, 40, *40*
 artificial lighting, 27
 bright sunny rooms, 26
lignification, 34
Ligustrum, 26
 L. sinensis (Chinese privet), 97, *97*
lime, in water, 41
lime-sulphur compound, 68, 69
liquid fertilizers, 42, 56
liverworts, 23

M

magnesium, 23, 55
mail order, 22-3
Malus (crab apple), 28, 57, 98, *98*
manure, farmyard, 47, 55
maples, 24, 37, 40, 56
 Japanese (*Acer palmatum*), 19, 29, 36, 43, 52-4, 73, *73*
 Japanese red (*Acer palmatum* "Deshojo/Chishio"), 40, 75, *75*
 Kiyohime (*Acer palmatum* "Kiyohime"), 74, *74*
 trident (*Acer buergerianum*), 25, 29, 72, *72*
Metropolitan Art Museum, Tokyo, 15
molybdenum, 55
moss, on soil, 23
Murraya, 26
 M. paniculata (jasmine orange), 99, *99*
Myrtus (myrtle), 27
 M. apiculata, 100, *100*

N
Nandina domestica (sacred bamboo), 27, 101, *101*
needle juniper (*Juniperus rigida*), 28, *94*, 95
needles, 36
    junipers, 61, *62*
    pines, 62-4
nitrogen, 55, 56-7
nitrogen-free fertilizers, 57
north-facing rooms, 27
nurseries, 18, *18*, *19*, 22, *22*, 23, *23*
nutrients:
    absorption by roots, 32, 33
    storage in roots, 33

O
Olea europea (olive), 18, 26, 102, *103*
organic fertilizers, 55-6
organic matter, soil, 46-7, *46*
osmosis, 32
outdoor bonsai, 19
    over winter *121*, 121
overhead watering, 42

P
Paris Exhibition (1937), 17
peat, 46, 47
penjing, 12
pests, 23
petioles, 36
phloem, 33, 35
phosphates, 56, 57
phosphorus, 55
photosynthesis, 36, 40
phytopthera, 41
Picea, 28
pigments, leaf color, 37
pinching out new growth, 61-5, *61 3*
Pinus (pines), 17, 40, 54, 57, 62-5, *64*, 67, 69
    P. parviflora (white pine), 24, 28, 104, *104*
    P. pentaphylla (white pine), 104, *104*
    P. thunbergii (Japanese black pine), *15*, 24, 28, 105, *105*
Pistacia terebinthus (pistachio), *16*, 18, 26, 106, *106*
plastic-coated iron wire, 67
Podocarpus, 26, *26*
    P. microphyllus (Chinese yew), 107, *107*
pomegranate (*Punica granatum*), 18, 26, 108, 109
pores, leaves, 36

Port Jackson fig, 17
potash, 33, 56, 57
potassium, 33, 55
potbound trees, watering, 42
pots:
    choosing, 52-4, *52-5*
    repotting, 48-51, *48*
potting composts, 46
privet, Chinese (*Ligustrum sinensis*), 97, *97*
pruning:
    branches, 60-1, *60*
    pinching out new growth, 61-5, *61-3*
    roots, 33, 48-9, *49*
pumice, crushed, 47
Punica granatum (pomegranate), 18, 26, *108*, 109
Pyracantha (firethorn), 28, 57, 110, *110*

Q
quince, flowering (*Chaenomeles*), 28, 82, *82*

R
rainwater, 41
regeneration pruning, 61
repotting, 48-51, *48*
Rhododendron indicum (Satsuki azalea), 62, 111, *111*
river sand, 47
roots, 32-3, *32-3*
    anchorage, 32
    breathing, 46
    buying bonsai, 23
    fertilizers, 56
    indoor bonsai, 24
    nutrient storage, 33
    outdoor bonsai, 24
    pruning, 33, 48-51, *49*
    repotting, 48-51, *48*
    root burn, 33
    root hairs, 32
    root stocks, 24
    watering, 42

S
sacred bamboo (*Nandina domestica*), 27, 101, *101*
Sageretia, 27
    S. theezans, *16*, 112, *112*
sand, 46, 47
sap, creating jins and sharis, 68-9
sapwood, 34
Satsuki azalea (*Rhododendron indicum*), 62, 111, *111*

scales, buds, 36
scars *see* wounds
scissors, 62
scorched leaves, 40, *40*
Scots pine, 17
sealants, wounds, 60
Serissa, 26, 54
    S. foetida (tree of a thousand stars), 113, *113*
shade, 36
shaded gardens, 29
shape, 24-5
    choosing pots, 52
    wiring, 65, 66-7
sharis, 67-8, *67*, 69
shoots:
    cambium, 34, *35*
    pinching out new growth, 61-2, *61*
slow-release fertilizers, 56
slugs, 43
snails, 43
soil, 46-7
    air spaces, 46
    conditioners, 47, *47*
    drainage, 41, *41*, 46, 50, 51
    mixing your own, 46-7, *47*
    repotting, 48, 50, 51
    types, 46, *46*
    water retention, 46, 47
    watering, 41, 42-3
south-facing rooms, 26
specialty nurseries, 23
spider mites, 23
Stewartia, 29, *29*
    S. monadelpha, 114, *114*
stomata, 36
Stuartia (*Stewartia monadelpha*), 114, *114*
sugars:
    autumn colors, 37
    phloem, 35
    photosynthesis, 36
sunlight, 28, 36, 40
sunny gardens, 28
sunny rooms, 26

T
Taiwan, 18
tapwater, 41
tools 122-123, *122*, *123*
trace elements, 23, 55, 56
transplanting, 33
trauma, bud production, 36-7
tree of a thousand stars (*Serissa foetida*), 113, *113*
trident maple (*Acer buergerianum*),

25, 29, 72, *72*
trunk, 34-5
    choosing pots, 52
    repotting, 51
    shape, 24
    sharis, 67-8, *67*, 69
turning bonsai, 40
tweezers, 61

U
Ulmus, 28
    U. parvifolia (Chinese elm), 26, 115, *115*
United States of America, 17

W
water:
    absorption by roots, 323
    drainage, 46, *50*, 51
    water softeners, 41
    watering, 40-3, *42*
    waterlogging, 46
waxy coating, leaves, 36
west-facing rooms, 26
white pine (*Pinus parviflora*), 24, 28, 104, *104*
winds, 43
wire cutters, 66
wiring:
    branches, *65*, 66-7
    repotting, 51
    scars, 24, *25*, 66, *66*
Wisteria, 28, 116, *116*
World War Two, 17
wounds:
    buying bonsai, 23, 245
    cambium, 34, *35*
    pruning branches, 60, *60*

X
xylem, 32-3, 34-5

Y
yellowing leaves, 23
yews, 29, 54
    Chinese (*Podocarpus microphyllus*), 107, *107*

Z
Zelkova, 29, 52-4
    Z. serrata (gray bark elm), *14*, 117, *117*
Zen religion, 14
zinc, 55

BONSAI – A CARE MANUAL

128

ACKNOWLEDGMENTS

The publishers would like to thank Peter Chan at Heron Bonsai and Charlotte Dalampira at Tokonoma Bonsai
for all their help in providing bonsai trees for photography

Bridgeman Art Library /Fitzwilliam Museum, University of Cambridge 13; Peter Chan /Herons 18, 19 bottom, 19 top; Corbis U.K. Ltd. /Bettman 14 bottom E.T. Archive /Victoria & Albert Museum 17; Garden Picture Library /David Askham 78 top, /Christopher Fairweather 82 right, /J.S. Sira 116 top, /Brigitte Thomas 34 bottom; Colin Lewis 9, 35, 119, 120, 121; Reed International Books Ltd. /Peter Myers/Herons 14 top, 20 /21, 22, 25 bottom, 52, 53, 54 bottom, 54 top, 55 right, 55 top left, 55 bottom left, 72, 73, 74, 75 left, 80 right, 80 left, 82 left, 83, 84, 86, 89, 91, 92, 93, 95 , 98 left, 103 , 104 , 108 , 110 , 111 , 114 , 115 , 116 bottom, 117 , /Peter Myers/Colin Lewis 1 , 2 /3, 4 /5, 10 /11, 21 inset, 24 bottom, 24 top, 30 /31, 31 inset, 32 bottom, 32 top, 36 top, 36 above center, 36 below center, 36 bottom, 38 /39, 40 bottom, 40, 41 top, 41 bottom, 42, 44/45, 46 top, 46 bottom, 46 center, 47 top, 47 bottom, 48 bottom, 48 top, 49 top, 49 bottom, 50 top, 50 bottom, 51 bottom, 51 top, 58 /59, 59 inset, 60, 61 bottom, 61 top, 61 center, 62 center, 62 top, 63, 64 bottom, 64 top, 65 above center, 65 bottom, 65 below center, 65 top, 66 right, 66 top, 66 below center, 66 above center, 66 bottom, 67, 68 top, 68 center, 68 bottom, 69 top, 69 center, 69 bottom, 70 /71, 75 right, /Peter Myers/Colin Lewis 51 center, /Peter Myers/Tokonoma/Sandie Long 81, /Peter Myers endpapers, 6 /7, 43 top, 109, 118 /119, /Peter Myers/Tokonoma 23, 77, 78 bottom, 79, 88, 90, 96, 97, 99, 100, 101, 102, 106, 107, 112, 113, 122 center right, 122 left, 122 top right, 122 bottom right, 123 center, 123 bottom, 123 top, /George Wright 34 top; Photos Horticultural 43 bottom; Harry Smith Collection 98 right